tricks, the small cruelties of boys and eventually Scott moves into more dangerous territory. I held my breath for him. With remarkable reticence, he comments very sparingly, leaving the reader in suspense as to what he's thinking. When I was finished reading, I wanted to ask him, "Well, then what happened?"

— Norita Dittberner-Jax, author of *World Enough and Time, New and Selected Poems*

"Long before Homer Simpson's D'oh! emerged to capture the lucid moment when one finds oneself deep in doo-doo, Scott Vetsch chronicled the hapless misdeeds of his childhood friends, parents, fellow poets, and of course himself. From the titular story of a date cursed by motion sickness to watching with horror as a skunk enters his tent in the middle of the night, Tilt-A-Whirl is a hilarious, self-deprecating ride into the awkward world of sexual awakening and experiments gone wrong that none of us ever completely leaves behind."

— Lynette Reini-Grandell, author of *Wild Things*

"Scott Vetsch's prose speaks from the heart of a Midwestern boy growing up in the 70s. More poetry than prose, packed with spoken imagery, light-hearted with a dark undercurrent. Words leap from the page and before long the reader is consumed by the narrative and taken for a mad carnival ride on the tilt-a-whirl of his youth. Step in line, buy your ticket, and enjoy the journey."

—Michael Hall, author of the *Spam River Journal*

"Tilt-A-Whirl" is a poignant coming-of-age collection of prose that spins through the dizzying highs and gut-wrenching lows of adolescence. Meet Scott Vetsch, a fiercely witty poet who navigates the complexities of friendship, identity, and the bittersweet journey of growing up.

Get ready to laugh out loud, even in moments of sorrow and struggle, at the wisdom Vetsch gleans from the messiness of parents, love, turtles, summer camp, the Vietnam War, and the Beatles. "Tilt-A-Whirl" invites readers to remember, life is a beautiful ride."

—Rosetta Peters, author of *The Hummingbird's Dance*

"Scott Vetsch writes with an owl's field of vision and the eye of an osprey. His is an experienced eye, like that of a hunter who can track fish underwater. You immediately know that he has examined the confusing currents, which exist beneath the surface of these emotionally raw and detailed vignettes. In anyone else's hands, these would become mere, nostalgic, or comical memories of his youthful, masculine life. With Vetsch these experiences emerge as non-judgemental and poignant, true-to-life prose poems. They carry the sensorial excitements, joys, defeats, and confusions of life spinning and lurching towards soulful maturity. They are a logbook for a 20th century journey to adulthood. When you find a poet like Vetsch, who writes with such clarity, detail, understanding, and compassion, you become one of earth's luckiest readers."

—Tim Young, author of *Memory's Honey-Cloud*

Praise for *Tilt-A-Whirl*

"These stories are NOT the same old thing.
Scott Vetsch has an eye and an ear for the things the rest of us missed.
For me, reading Scott's stories is a series of 'Aha' moments.
'Oh yeah.' 'Of Course.' 'Why didn't I see that before?'
As a raconteur, Scott Vetsch is one of the Best.
I love Tilt-A-Whirl. You will too."

— Ted King, author of *Modern Problems*

"This book is classic Americana by a professionally-laidback guy who still nods about his first transistor radio's unwillingness to tune in much from faraway, and his natural ability to see that "the world was on fire, and Doris Day's face was still out of focus."

Of the hundreds of autobiographical and waking up to the world stories I've read, I remember only a handful (by William Saroyan, Robert Paul Smith, Jean Shephard) that blend angst, wonder, confusion, fear, hope (Everything!) as skillfully and unpretentiously as in this tilt-a-whirling collection by Scott Vetsch.

These stories about growing up in rural Minnesota aren't romanticized or mucked up with what-I-know-now commentary. They're kind and so engagingly clear that the reader never feels manipulated or reproached with anything but Scott's rare downhome honesty (yeah, it's rare) that welcomes you to dig a hole to China, go to Bobo's Creek, try a cigarette for the first time, or drop acid with him. All to a rising threat of a faraway war and a rising promise of rock & roll in the background."

— Tom Cassidy, author of *From The Scenic Outlook the Battlefield Churns Beautifully*

"In the prose-poem stories of *Tilt-A-Whirl*, his memories of family, friends, small town life find Scott Vetsch like recurring dreams. They teach him to face his fears, navigate the rebellion and dangers of adolescence. "I loved heights, but motion killed me." He sees the world through the innocence of his younger self. Hearing Jim Morrison singing on the hockey-rink radio was "scorching the fences that divided me from myself." Yet, compassion for smaller lives—turtles, a field mouse, fish, June bugs—and fear of death are just under the surface. Hearing a neighbor is not returning from Viet Nam, he wonders, "when it would be my turn?" The subtle humor and irony in these memoir/parables offer him the possibility of forgiveness, healing, joy, freedom. For Scott Vetsch, these true stories are about "calibrating your soul's compass," a way to understand life. This book is a delight!"

— Michael S. Moos, author of *The Idea of the Garden*

"scott vetsch writes like the guy you met wandering nepal, the guy who ended up with two kids by a tibetan nun, living for ten years in the foothills of the Himalayas. later on he landed in rural northern wisconsin and farmed alfalfa, raised goats, and made cheese for his living. nights he mostly wrote poems down at the village dive bar and played pull tabs til closing."

— Dougie Padilla, author of *Forty Feet Down*

"In *Tilt-A-Whirl*, Scott Vetsch tells his own coming-of-age story with all the ups and downs of a real life tilt-a-whirl. 1967, the boy at 7 or 8 plays hockey with friends who will grow up with him in the neighborhood. There is a freshness to Vetsch's narrative voice. It's straight-forward and insightful and full of details that the reader will remember from those years: merit badges, Hamburger Helper, bras designed like armor. So much mischief,

Tilt-A-Whirl

CALUMET EDITIONS
Minneapolis

FIRST EDITION APRIL 2025
Tilt-A-Whirl Copyright © 2025 by Scott Edward Vetsch.
All rights reserved.

No part of this book may be used or reproduced in any manner whatsoever without written permission except in the case of brief quotations used in critical articles and reviews. For information, write to Calumet Editions, 6800 France Ave. S., Suite 370, Minneapolis, MN 55435

10 9 8 7 6 5 4 3 2 1
ISBN: 978-1-962834-38-4

Cover and interior design: Gary Lindberg

Tilt-A-Whirl

A Memoir

Scott Vetsch

Minneapolis

Dedicated with all my love to those
who were there and to Julia

Table of Contents

A Kid's-eye View of the Lizard King   1

Quicksand   3

Trapping Snappers   5

It's Always an Old Man   7

Horse Sense   9

The Vulcan   11

Toad Swamp   13

Mowing the Grass   17

Digging to China   19

Marbles   23

The Spawning Grounds   25

Children of the Revolution   31

The Kite   35

Serpentine   39

The Wheel   43

Love Letter to Wrassling   47

The Walrus   51

The Fifth Horseman   57

Instructions   59

The Great Leap Forward   61

Dad's Lesson   63

The Camping Craze   65

The Night the Revolution Came Home   67

Ghosts   71

Military Industrial Complex   75

Cat In the Sack   81

Going for a Can of Coke   83

Fun Facts Club   85

Tilt-A-Whirl   93

Wash Under Your Shorts, Boys   97

Addressing Mister Bader   103

Viva Zapata   105

The Fetterman Switcheroo   107

Boyhood Distractions   111

Loop-O-Plane   113

The Great Escape   115

Sharp Tits   117

The Day Brent's Brothers Jumped Off the Bridge   121

The First of Many Choices Based On Love   123

An Education   125

Army Men   129

Mechanics of the First Kiss   133

Smoking   137

Anthropology   141

160 Carp   143

Hickeys Were Part of the Problem   147

The Grizzly Adams of Advertising   153

Hiking Merit Badge   155
Mill Pond 1975   159
Men's Room Reflections   161
Junebug   163
Parental Advice   165
Tripping by the Bridge   167
A Scout is Reverent   169
Postcard from the Bicentennial Summer   173
I Never Wanted to Be That Guy   175
Coming of Age   179
Joining the Tribe   181
Coat Pile   183
Finding the Faithful Pony Within   185
A Civics Lesson   187
Between the Lines in '79   189
Wrecked   191
About the Author   199

Also by Scott Vetsch

Bullhead Country
(a book of poetry and prose)

A Kid's-eye View of the Lizard King

If I cared enough to imagine what a poet looked like, it came from Disney; a bookish, bespectacled wretch hunched over a table, scratching rhymes on paper. Tortured, benign, certainly no danger to society. Poetry was a category, like bowling or ballet, something that people did, but not vital.

No boy set out to become that wretch. Where I come from boys worked on engines, or played football; poetry was something that got your ass kicked.

I asked the pastor in Sunday school why no one believed a guy who claimed he could heal the lame or make the blind see. He said it was because the bible was written in the Age of Miracles and miracles just didn't happen anymore.

In the winter of '67, I joined the hockey team. We practiced every evening at the village skating rink. On those crisp black, sub-zero nights, the hockey rink was an island of light. A speaker was screwed to the warming house wall, radio tuned to KDWB, our schoolyard alive with the soundtrack of revolution. "Light My Fire" cast its hypnotic spell on me. It spawned a yearning I couldn't name, before returning home to a plate of tuna hotdish.

I heard his voice, then found his face in *Life* Magazine.

Dark eyes and bare chest, brown curls falling around his face, the rest encased in leather. Jim stole poetry back from the teachers. Stood the poet up in front of an audience like a god and made him dangerous. Made the poem physical, made sexuality cinematic.

This was the kind of poet I wanted to be. Not a New England-type kenneled in some Ivy League college, but one who lived on the highway as far as that car would go. He made poetry young again, gave it libido. He didn't call it rock-n-roll, he said it was poetry, and not that hobbled version we learned in school. This poetry didn't live in your head, like they taught you. You found it in your body .

Jim wasn't some fossil from the Age of Miracles. He was a warrior poet, scorching the fences that divided me from myself.

Quicksand

A wagon creaking across the desert suddenly found itself sinking in bottomless muck that looked exactly like the sand around it. Soon the spoked wooden wheels were down to their axles, a man up to his chin: requiring the toss of a cowboy's lariat.

I asked Grandpa about quicksand. He said it was an underground spring that percolated loose soil, suspended it, filled the space between each grain of sand. The springs flow kept it in motion.

I heard what he said, but saw only a cowboy's panicked expression, sinking beneath a black and white movie set, as fantastic as *The Creature from the Black Lagoon*.

Grandpa didn't watch television except for the news and *All-Star Wrestling*.

He told me about bogs, said to stay out of 'em. They were floating islands that grew across a lake and looked like land. He said it was springy and undulated when you walked on it, like waves on a lake. If you slipped between the matted roots, there was only water beneath you. If you fell through, you might not find that same hole when you came back up, and you'd drown.

He said behind Jack Callahan's was a place called Cartwheel Woods; a quarter section of oak hills and tamarack bog. Grandma said the people who owned it didn't live there.

Cartwheel Woods. Clearly it was named after at least one wagon sunk in that treacherous quicksand. It was also pretty close to Cartwright, the name of the family that owned The Ponderosa on *Bonanza*.

Grandpa made me swear I'd never go in there, but I could already see the ghostly wrecks bleaching in the sun. I pushed him for details. How many wagons were sunk in there? Had he ever seen human skulls? Or a skeleton?

We drove by that woods as long as I could remember, but now it had a name and was bubbling with quicksand. That night, I found some paper and drew a map with X's and dotted lines on it, imagining the quicksand and all the wreckage it concealed.

Trapping Snappers

Grandpa agreed to help Maynard haul a load of turtles to market, and I rode along.

He drove the red, sun-faded, '49 Chevy pick-up with the running boards that ended each fender like a smile.

Everybody said Maynard's wife was a gypsy.

They lived in a chicken coop, at the end of a narrow road through the woods where Omsrud Lake lapped at its marshy shore.

When we got there, Maynard was waist deep in the water, pulling on his hog-wire turtle trap. Grandpa backed down to the muddy beach and together they loaded snapping turtles into the truck box. The smaller ones they carried by the tail, one in each hand.

The big ones Maynard goaded with a stick to bite.

They don't let go once they strike, so Grandpa grabbed the tail, Maynard held the stick, and together they heaved it over the tailgate.

Sitting in the middle, stick-shift between my knees, I turned to watch that crawling pile of turtles through the back window. We drove to Mankato and backed into the loading dock of a meat market where Maynard sold them. Grandpa said they were headed for a French restaurant that served frog-legs and turtle soup.

It's Always an Old Man

We were driving home from Grandma's when I confessed to Mom I hadn't pooped the whole time we were there. Our Galaxy 500's black interior was hot with the summer sun, passenger compartment filled with cigarette smoke. Dad was behind the wheel listening to a ball game. Mom turned around in the front seat.

This wasn't the first time this conversation came up. I was the oldest child. Mom's toilet training was rigorous, by the book, but I chose to believe I could avoid the whole thing. It was where my procrastination began. I fought each battle knowing I would lose the war, but could postpone it, tomorrow was another day.

Mom's response was measured, she said there was an old man she remembered, when she was a kid. He didn't go to the bathroom for a whole year, but when he finally did, it came out of his mouth.

I sank into a peristaltic meditation. Another time Mom had told me about an old man whose entire house was picked up by a tornado and set down across the road, completely intact. I wondered if this was the same guy.

I imagined him wearing a prospector's hat, a grizzled beard from yesteryear, his stance wide in surprise, engulfed by that final eruption, and I wondered if he used toilet paper or a napkin.

Horse Sense

I was staying at my Grandparents. We'd just come back from Harold's Poke 'N' Tote, where they bought me a toy horse. I needed to name it.

A song by The Association, "Windy", was on the radio a lot, "Her eyes flash stormy at the sound of lies." It was a perfect, speedy name for a horse. I told Grandpa I was calling her Windy.

He chuckled and said it was a funny name for a horse. I asked why. He just smiled.

Grandpa grew up in a horse world. He broke broncos for a buck apiece before he met Grandma and farmed with teams of horses more than half his life. So I wanted to know what was wrong, why it was funny.

He laid it out like a parable, told me you didn't wanna ride behind a windy horse.

I was pretty sure I knew what he was talking about, but the name was too good. I fought back with a twentieth century mindset.

"What if you didn't hook him up to a wagon?" I said, "What if you rode him? Wouldn't it help, like a jet engine?"

The Vulcan

My sister, my mom and I were huddled together on Main Steet in Anoka, watching the Halloween parade. I was no taller than Mom's elbow, so I had a good view of what happened when the Vulcan went after her.

He was dressed in his devil costume, hood and horns around his sooty black grease-painted face. He had his arms around her, and I wondered if Mom knew who was under that disguise. Was it someone's dad from church? A member of the Lion's Club? Mr. Perdle from the shoe store, all lit up, testing his mettle?

I could smell the alcohol on his breath, see him crush his face to hers in a rough kiss. Mom's arm swung back in a discrete arc. She punched him sharply in the solar plexus and I watched him deflate.

"Git Goin'." she said.

Toad Swamp

Sweazy and I got off the school bus at our stop in his grandma's driveway. It was Friday afternoon, snow melted, green pushing through the yellow. There was a stand of dead sumac at the edge of the woods, clattering, gnarly and black. Their trunks were an inch or so across and if you pushed hard, they snapped off at the base.

We built a wigwam, resting the dead stalks together at the peak, going around, filling it in with more, leaving space for a door we could crawl inside. It was an odd place to hang out, by the road, overlooking a ditch, but we resolved to work on it again the next day.

Saturday morning, we made peanut butter sandwiches, found a few carrots in the fridge, and some little boxes of Sun-Maid raisins. We didn't have a backpack like we imagined, so we dumped out his brother's erector-set box to put our lunch in because it looked like a tin suitcase. We carried it back to the bus-stop.

It was early in the day, Meadow Larks still singing. The wigwam was pretty much done, already losing its magic to the bus-stop and the smell of last year's brown leaves.

Hauling the Erector-Set box, we climbed up the hill, crossed Indian Mound Road, and down the fence-line between Larson's and Fred Keniston's. Beyond their outbuildings were woods and fields. When we crossed the trickle of Oak Creek, we were further than we'd ever been. We walked 'til we came upon the far rows of a junkyard.

Rusty regiments of old cars, trucks and panel-vans wound toward the trees. Our only worry was a barking dog, but we figured it was chained because it didn't get any closer. We could climb into any cab, sit behind any wheel and drive deep into our imaginations. Then we heard frogs chirping.

We ran toward the sound, through tall grass and found a little pond screaming with frogs. We rolled up our pants and went in with our sneakers. After we caught a few, we realized they were all toads; talk about segregation, not a frog among them.

We named it Toad Swamp on all subsequent maps of our territory. It was a landmark, like the Mill Pond or the Mississippi River.

With a toad in each hand, we dumped our lunch on the ground and slid em into the box.

We caught more toads that morning than ever in our lives and carried them home like the spoils of war.

The Erector-Set box was never reunited with its pieces. It ended up teetering on a bushel-basket of broken toys in the corner of Lofton's garage, empty, except for the rusty imprints of toads etched across its bottom.

Mowing the Grass

The Leinfelders lived across the road. There were lots of kids in the family, boys and girls in nearly every grade from kindergarten to high school. Leanne, the youngest, was my age; Bill was a senior.

His hair was sandy brown, combed to the side. He wore those black-framed glasses like Dennis the Menace's dad. He mowed our lawn because Mom couldn't, now that my sister was a toddler.

One day I noticed his younger brother Roger mowing the grass and asked Mom why. She said Bill had been drafted into the army, gone to Vietnam.

A lot of boys were going to Vietnam. On the nightly news Walter Cronkite and David Brinkley told us how many died.

When we heard Bill wasn't coming back, I thought about Roger mowing the grass, filling the space left by his brother, how he might feel about that, and wondered when it would be my turn.

Digging to China

In kindergarten someone told us, if you dug down deep enough, really deep, you'd come out in China. It didn't seem possible. I already knew about the earth's fiery core, something I imagined as the perfectly round center of a Superball containing an orange nougat of molten lava. I understood the planet was really big, just digging a tunnel to Grandma's with a shovel would take years.

After school, Sweazy and I were talking to Mom and wondered: If you could dig through the earth, when you came out the other side, would you be upside down? Mom said compared to here you would, but it would feel like up. She said the earth was always turning and everyone on it looked up at the sky. So we figured if you dug a hole and kept digging, at a certain depth, down switched to up.

We ran to the shed, grabbed a spade, and started digging. Mom let me use an empty flower bed below the kitchen window for my dump trucks and army men.

We pushed them aside and took turns digging, soon there was a hole and a pile of dirt.

Mom watched out the window whenever she was at the sink. She was cooking supper, happy we were occupied. We kept digging, pushing, wondering how deep we'd have to go before down was up? If we broke through, would we fall up, cause right now the bottom of the hole was definitely down. I expected trouble at the earth's core but figured we had a ways to go before we had to worry about it.

Grandpa and Grandma were coming to supper, and when they showed up at the backdoor, they asked what we were doing. "Digging to China!" we answered. "Be sure and greet those Chinamen for me," Grandpa replied, and went inside.

I visualized barefoot farmers hoeing in their fields, wearing those round pointy straw hats like the Vietnamese we saw on the evening news. We wondered, if a Chinaman dug toward us, would he fall past into the sky when he broke through?

The hole was up to our waists, past the black topsoil into yellow clay; possibility drove us deeper. The next time I saw Mom through the window she didn't look happy, she must've heard about our plans.

Not long after, Grandpa came out to examine our quest. He said he'd hand dug a few wells when he was younger, told us if you stood in the bottom at midday, you could see the stars in the sky just like it was night.

"Wow... how deep do you have to go to see that?"

"Pretty deep." Grandpa said. He picked up the shovel and leaned on it. He was a farmer, but this night was wearing a white shirt and black dress pants. It was weird to see him all dressed up holding that shovel.

"Before you get to China," Grandpa explained, "You'll probably hit an underground river."

"Really? What happens then?"

"Well," he answered, "You know the Grain Belt beer commercial, that geyser of water shooting out of the ground? That's an artesian well--an underground river. Once you uncover it, even just bust through with a shovel, it'll rise up like Old Faithful. No stopping it then."

"Really, right here!?"

It was a sleight of hand, Grandpa was filling in the hole as he explained springs, seeps, and artesian wells and we didn't even care, that image of the Grain Belt Beer fountain kept us mesmerized.

"How do you know where an underground river is?"

Grandpa told us about divining rods and witching for water. He had the hole completely filled in, tamping it down with the flat of the spade, by the time Mom stood on the porch in her apron smiling, saying it was time to eat. China was a distant memory, but we knew after supper, we'd scour the woods for forked sticks.

Marbles

Mom sewed my first marble bag from a blue washcloth folded in half and stitched together. Unfortunately, she made the drawstring opening, not how I wanted on the short side, but down the long side, so all my marbles rolled to one side like misshapen testes.

I saved up my allowance and bought a brown and black leather marble bag at Ben Franklin. It was one that other kids had, something I could carry outside my pants.

On the compacted dirt of the elementary school playground, we played for keeps, following our marbles underneath the slippery slide or around the monkey bars. There were regular-sized marbles, shooters, and half-shooters. There were cat-eyes, peeries, and steelies. Steelies were ball bearings and some kids' dads were mechanics or worked in machine shops; some possessed steelies the size of baseballs.

The rest of us dreamed of winning one, but they'd only play you for a peery shooter.

These guys weren't collectors; theirs was a game of attrition. After you missed, their turn fell like an asteroid pulverizing your peery into icy shards.

Nothing remained but walking away.

The Spawning Grounds

There were northerns in the creek. Dad said they had to be coming down from Hayden Lake. Hayden was a swampy lake; the creek ran through it a couple miles upstream. You could see it on the map, but there was no access, no view; only willows and marsh grass.

Dad was sure they were spawning up there somewhere, by deduction the conditions were perfect: isolated, shallow, extensive and weedy, inlet and outlet at each end.

The mythical spawning ground grew in Dad's imagination like some treasure map scrawled on a beer coaster.

Dad chose a Saturday in June for our expedition. He usually worked weekends, photographing weddings, but fish bite in the morning and his wedding was at 2pm. It wasn't more than a mile to drive and Dad figured we'd be on the water at sunup, have our limit and be loaded out by ten.

The only way into Hayden was to enter downstream. Dad enlisted his buddy Ron to man the bow. The night before we tied the canoe onto our '64 Galaxy, stowed the gear in the trunk, and bought minnows at the gas station. I was so excited I kicked over the bucket on the driveway and we scooped them up by the wriggling handful coated in grit. Dad was mad, said it would kill 'em. I could barely sleep, and when the alarm rang at five, Dad was right, half were dead.

There was a bend we fished in the creek that Dad called the northern hole. It was always good for a couple, and we hadn't been skunked yet. Kids in school called it BoBo's, after the dog that lived in the yellow house perched high on the southern bank.

Dad parked on the road, and we carried the canoe and equipment through the brush, got the boat in the water, loaded up and pushed off. Past Bobo's, the tunnel of trees receded, and the sky opened. We were out in the sun, banks dropping, reeds filling the edges. Once we portaged the flood control dam at the outlet it was all new to me.

Sun at our backs, we paddled out. On each side cattails and bulrushes rose overhead, an impenetrable wall of green tagged with the perching trills of redwing blackbirds.

In the distance there was open water, but as we advanced it began to narrow. We should have been approaching the lake and Dad wondered if we'd missed it. The deeper we followed the channel, the narrower it became, until it was just an alley leaning against our shoulders.

The sun was moving higher into the blue sky, coolness departing, stagnation rising. There was a sense of unease as the water retreated ahead. The promising course we followed vanished into a uniformity of bulrushes. Paddling had gone from poling to strained heaving. Digging their paddles into the bottom, they pushed together, levered our hull, screeching and scratching through the muck.

Finally, comfort and expedience parted ways. I'd been hoping at each moment, that we'd break into a clearing and find northerns swirling and basking like manatees in the shallows of some secret pool, but there wasn't enough water for anything but frogs. Ron stood up in the bow but couldn't see over the tops of the vegetation. It became easier to get out and drag the canoe forward than continue pushing through the mud. Dad dumped the rest of the minnows without a word.

Each mud-sucking step released blurps of stagnant swamp stink. It was too sunny for mosquitos, but the slop kicked up the deerflies.

The humidity was thick. I was wearing my blue Jack Purcell's. I never wore socks and my ankles were burning. I lifted one out of the water and saw they were bleeding; crisscrossed with hundreds of little cuts and scratches from the sharp edges of the bulrushes. Dad was wearing his white high-tops and they gripped his ankles, but after one unusually deep suctioning step, my right foot came out of the mud without its shoe.

I assumed it was lost forever, but Dad wasn't ready to admit defeat. Who knew how much walking we had ahead of us; a seven-year-old without a shoe was going to be a problem, plus he'd be the one buying a new pair.

Thigh deep in the mud, I showed him the hole that stole my shoe. Dad crouched on his hands and knees, reached his arm down shoulder deep, cheek pillowed in the muck. He groped around 'til he got a hold of it, braced himself against the suction, and like some infernal midwife, wrenched out a great stinking ball of mud, and slipped it back on my foot.

The sun was moving toward its zenith, and we were lost and that realization filled Dad with anxiety. A compass bearing of due west was no guarantee Dad would reach his 2pm wedding, showered and shaved.

He helped me climb up on his shoulders to spy a landmark, but I still couldn't see over the rush-tops. To make better time, Ron and I divvied up the gear: fishing poles, life jackets, minnow bucket, paddles, and landing net. Dad upturned the canoe over his head and all the muck that had been sloshing around on the bottom drizzled down over his head and shoulders.

We plodded on for a while 'til he set the canoe down and had me climb up on his shoulders again to reconnoiter. This time I spied the distant leafy branches of a willow, and overjoyed, we set off with renewed confidence. Suddenly, like an oasis, we saw the mowed backyard of a house bordering the swamp.

A woman was kneeling with her back to us, working in her garden. Dad told us to wait in the weeds, he'd walk up and ask directions. Parting the vegetation, he stumbled into the open. I felt like we'd been rescued; mown grass never looked so good. The garden was a distance up the hill and as Dad approached, he called out. She turned and quickly scrambled to her feet. Dad was splotched and filthy, black hair plastered to his head, mud and algae running down his face.

He shambled toward her laughing. She headed toward the house. I wouldn't call it running, but definitely a power walk. When she reached her door, she stepped inside and shut it. Dad followed her up and knocked. She cracked it open, asked what he wanted.

"You probably think I'm crazy," Dad said, "well maybe I am."

She wasn't amused. He told her about our canoeing fiasco and asked to use the phone. She wouldn't let him in the house. People often escaped from the Anoka Mental Hospital; she didn't see any boat. She told him what road went by out front. He asked if he could come back with his car and pick up the canoe. She said sure.

Ron and I sat in the cattails. Eventually Dad's red Ford pulled into the driveway, and we started hauling gear up the hill. Dad and Ron carried the mud-smeared canoe up and set it on the roof-racks. The lady came out. She didn't think Dad had escaped from the mental hospital anymore, but she still didn't like it.

Turns out we were just down the road from where we parked that morning. When we got home and pulled into the turnaround, Mom was waiting on the porch. As we climbed out of the car, caked in mud, Mom's arms crossed over her chest, like when my frogs got loose in the house.

Dad showered off the muck and got to his wedding, but swamp stink is like marriage, 'til death do you part.

Children of the Revolution

In 1968 I was in the third grade. It was Mrs. Opinski's first year teaching. To help us remember her name she turned to the chalkboard and drew a big O, plus a small safety pin, plus the bent shape of a ski. She wore a pageboy, no makeup.

A couple months into the term she announced to the class that her husband had been sent to Vietnam.

My uncle was a chopper mechanic. A couple days before his unit deployed to Vietnam, he contracted pneumonia, and when he recovered, he lucked out and got stationed in Korea. I kept his graduation photo in the cowboy wallet I got for my birthday, slipped between the plastic sleeves that held my library card and other valued documents; a graduation photo of Mom's cousin Sonja in her mesmerizing beehive hairdo and a snapshot of my other uncle in his National Guard uniform; someone had to stay home and milk the cows.

On the bus ride home in the afternoons I would meditate on those photographs. I had no photograph of my father, but had his name, and prayed no one would ever mistake me for his son or see him in my face. The photos of my uncles were my talisman against that; my father despised all things military.

One day Mrs. Opinski asked how many students had family serving in Vietnam. Lots of kids raised their hands. I was an oldest kid, had no older siblings, and was stunned how many did. I was even more surprised when I raised my hand along with them.

She asked each child with an arm up who it was. They replied "My Dad," or "My brother." When she got to me, I said, "Brother." Mrs. Opinski was surprised, "I didn't know you had a brother that old Scott, your mother seems so young." I shrugged but insisted. I hadn't considered age; my mother was 29.

A few days later Mrs. Opinski called my mother to voice her concern.

In the winter came an announcement that the husband we'd never seen was killed in action. We had a substitute teacher for a few weeks until she came back.

On the last day of school, she treated the entire class to ice cream. We walked the half-mile down to Tast-ee-Freez. I ordered a chocolate push-up.

Across the highway, an old bridge bright with peace symbols and psychedelic graffiti, spanned a narrows of the Mill Pond. Teens were swimming already, screaming, jumping and splashing. Summer had arrived, transistors and car radios played the music of revolt.

Eating our ice-cream on the way back to school, Mrs. Opinski bent to remove her shoes. She scooped them up with her free hand and walked on barefooted. Someone asked if we could take our shoes off too. She looked down at the warm tar, weeds pushing through the cracks, and said yes.

The Kite

One Sunday at the grocery store, I studied that end-of-the-aisle toy display while Mom shopped. There were four or five model cars and airplanes, bags of army men, plastic squirt guns, and cheap scary baby dolls that wet their diapers. My allowance was a dime and that made the choice easy unless I wanted to find Mom and beg, which never worked. I purchased a paper Jolly Roger kite with wood struts.

I unrolled it when I got home. There was no tail. Dad showed me how to make one from cut-up T-shirt scraps and a length of string. His instruction was to make it as long as it needed to be.

The ribbons of tied-on fabric didn't look like the pictures of kite-tails I'd seen in books; they weren't brightly colored bow-ties with crisp edges. They were lumpy and reminded me of Dad sitting around in his underwear. Disillusioned by uncertainty, I decided the tail was long enough and went outside. Dad was watching football on TV, Sunday papers scattered across the floor.

I laid the kite out on the grass, uncoiled a few yards of line and started running. It trailed behind at shoulder height, but the only passion it showed for flight was when it turned upside down and plowed into the ground. I'd have more luck dragging a pizza box into the air.

A couple years later I won a kite for selling Scout-O-Rama tickets. It wasn't anything I wanted, but better than a volleyball or a bell for my bicycle.

The Scout-O-Rama kite required no tail, it was tall and skinned with clear, rugged cellophane, silhouette of a red jet aircraft stenciled across its center. I snapped it together, tied on the line, took it outside, held it up and the sky pulled it from my hands. I didn't need to run, just stood there and the line reeled off.

The kite pulled on my arm like a dog wanting to run. I wound it back down, got on my bike and rode to the store. I decided on two balls of line, just in case.

I stopped at Sweazy's on the way home and told him about the kite. He came over to check it out. I held it up and it soared, pulling out line. I tied on another spool, tied on the next and it was gone in ten minutes. It looked like a real airplane up there. I was too old for such illusions, but it was still pretty cool.

Tilt-A-Whirl

By now, my little sister Nora was watching. To her it was grand. She still lived in the world where new sneakers gave you the power to run faster and jump higher. When she climbed a tree and leapt to the ground, she hoped to clear the treetops and leave it all behind. She raced through flocks of grackles, expecting to take flight as they rose around her.

Nora and Perry traded off holding the reins while Sweazy and I rode back to the store. Nora believed, hand over hand, you could climb that line to the kite. I knew that was impossible, but she was right about the feeling: A line cast to the clouds, bobber adrift, fishing for a world I couldn't reach.

We returned with four balls of string and added them on. The kite nearly disappeared, became a red dot. Even Dad, that harbinger of hopelessness, came home from work, stood on the porch, shadowed his eyes with a hand and said, "That's incredible."

I tied the string to the clothesline pole, like hitching a boat to the dock, and we all went home for supper. While Mom washed dishes, I dug through drawers and found another ball of string. Sweazy showed up with two more.

Dusk was falling and the kite had vanished, string stretched to infinity. Bats had begun their evening acrobatics overhead when Sweazy's parents walked over, following news of the mythical star. Our flag flew, a proclamation; claiming things we couldn't touch.

I wanted to leave it up there, make time stop, but I couldn't. I had to go to bed and get up for school. I realized this couldn't last forever. It would end up tangled in someone's TV antenna. If we pulled it down, we'd have it for another day.

I tied the line to a scrap of wood and started winding. The lump of string grew thicker, like a spider's web wrapped round a fly. Flashlight beams jotted across the sky like searchlights, Nora and Perry danced like primitives, like fireflies casting their glow. No one could believe how much line was on the stick and still no kite, until suddenly there it was, below the treetops. The adults declared it bedtime, the flashlights switched off, and everyone was reeled back home to their lives.

Serpentine

Mr. Clean was a product, a toilet cleaner. TV ads said it cleaned like a white tornado. Mr. Clean was a white guy with a shaven head and a big gold earring. I never figured out he was supposed to be a genie blasting out of a bottle to battle dirt and stains. I was more focused on the tornado part, a thing I was familiar with.

It was the summer of '66, a Saturday afternoon, and we were under a tornado watch, that terrible warning that blared from WCCO radio. It was a year after record floods and devastating tornados hit our region. We were primed for disaster.

The only genies I'd ever seen were on TV. They were turbaned and untrustworthy, might give you three wishes or cut off your head if you asked wrong. *I Dream of Jeanie* was Caucasian too, but there was nothing weird about that. All our gods and heroes were white, even if they really weren't. Mr. Clean should have looked more like Cassius Clay, not Yule

Brenner. But that's how we are. Like the empires before us, we take gods from the vanquished and make them our own.

I was looking out the kitchen window and Mom was doing dishes. The sun was shining, clouds puffy and thick. I thought I saw a finger-like shape descending in the direction of Osseo.

Tornados were like nuclear war, or the Abominable Snowman from *Rudolf the Red Nosed Reindeer*. It was something you didn't want to see, even though you kinda really did. The cloud finger was getting longer, but I didn't believe it, like the time we ran home and told our parents we saw a bear down by the river.

I said, "Mom...Is that a tornado?" She didn't look up, just replied, "I don't think so."

Dad was mowing the back yard. I saw him in the distance, crossing it with each swath he made. Mom looked up again, and suddenly, without a word, she was out the door, running toward him.

I was a kid, never right about anything. Through the window I saw Mom get Dad's attention. She pointed to the horizon, and I saw him turn, shade his eyes, and study the sky. I never saw Dad run, he wasn't a guy who was ever in that much of a hurry, but they were running now.

That was the moment I realized I was right.

It was a tornado, stretched out like a snake, reaching for the ground. The sun shone, and the tornado wasn't black and terrible like the ones I'd seen in books. It was white, like the one in the Mr. Clean commercial.

It hadn't touched the ground yet, wasn't full of dirt and debris, but I kinda wished it was, like that evening, days before Christmas, when I looked out that very window, to see the Fetterman's house on fire, flames shooting out the windows, burning as bright as a jack o lantern in the darkness. Mom said they weren't home, but I kinda wished they were, firemen kicking down the door, pulling them from the ruins. My fascination with catastrophe had to be content imagining their Christmas tree and all their presents destroyed.

That tornado never turned black, just slithered back into the clouds and left us, pretty much as we were. Mom went back to her dishes, Dad started the mower, and I kept watch, hoping it might come back.

The Wheel

It was Sunday afternoon, and we were working around the house. I was cleaning out the window wells when I discovered a field mouse and trapped it with a shoebox. All I wanted to do was have a look and let it go, but Dad said he had a friend with an empty hamster cage and volunteered to drive over and get it.

We watched the mouse 'til he came back. The cage was nice: enameled blue metal sides, bars top and front, and a wheel to run on. Mom gave me a carrot and some lettuce. That was the shock. Mom had always enforced a ban on rodents as pets, but it seemed this time, she wouldn't get in the way of Dad showing an interest in his children.

The mouse was a distraction, and no further chores were completed that day. Soon it was suppertime.

While Mom was washing dishes, we went back outside. It was a beautiful evening, twilight with a smell of mown grass, the flickering blue of TV's; neighborhood winding down, gearing up for another week of work.

I was imagining life with a pet mouse, maybe bring it to school for Show and Tell, just when Dad wondered why it wouldn't use the wheel.

I told him it didn't matter to me, I didn't care. It bothered Dad. He picked up the cage and shook the mouse toward the wheel. There were no wood shavings inside, just some newspaper, a dish of water, the carrot and the wilting lettuce. Vegetables and dish were rattling around, mouse scrabbling. Soon Dad had the cage upside down above his head, shaking the mouse toward the wheel.

Whenever the mouse grabbed the wheel. Dad stopped shaking. When it abandoned the wheel, the upheaval resumed. This went on for hours. Dad had intense concentration with things like this. My sister and I watched without emotion, mentioned we didn't care if the mouse used the wheel. But Dad was determined, said he was gonna make that mouse love the wheel, make it depend on the wheel.

We watched guiltily, numb, too cowardly to make a stand, relieved, because his attention was on the mouse, not us; a sacrificial lamb like our cat, sometimes each other. Dad knew all about wheels, if he had to be on one, everyone else did too.

Eventually the mouse clung to the wheel, the only stable thing it had and started running. I give Dad credit; when he set himself a goal, he achieved it.

The mouse kept running, I heard the wheel squeaking late into the night, long after I was in bed. The next morning it was quiet and I hoped the mouse was sleeping, but it was lying dead on the wheel. Mom said it must have run its little heart out.

Love Letter to Wrassling

There wasn't much Grandpa did that depended on a clock.

His schedule was determined by daylight or weather.

But on Saturday evenings, shirt-sleeves or flannel,

he had a date with *All-Star Wrestling*.

At five minutes to seven, he turned on the television and sat down,

elbows on knees, waiting for Marty O'Neil to start announcing

all the way from the Calhoun Beach Hotel.

Grandpa didn't follow football or hockey.

Spent time in his fields, or milking cows, or tending garden,

so I figured Wrassling was important too.

I watched with him but couldn't see the attraction.

It looked fakey. Of course there were things I watched

that were fakey too, but they were cartoons and I was a kid.

The world was supposed to be real.

This was a front row seat

to the flawed world of adults.

I asked Grandma if he knew it wasn't real,

but Grandma read the *National Enquirer*

for entertainment, she said;

what did she know about real.

She said Grandpa respected the wrestlers' athleticism, which meant the theatricality;

the jumping off the top rope,

the throwing of chairs,

the tantrums and the body slams.

Their names: Gorgeous George, Harley Race, Luscious Lars Anderson, Tiny Mills,

Mad Dog Vashon, Larry "The Axe" Henning, The Bruiser, The Crusher, Vern Gagne, Rick Bockwinkle, Hard Boiled Haggerty, Baron von Raschke, and Dr. X.

Each possessed an arsenal of holds:

the figure-four-leg-lock

the Pile Driver

the Claw

the Sleeper.

It was Cold War politics and tribal divisions.

My Grandfather had a sixth-grade education.

English was not his native tongue.

I loved him.

The Walrus

Christmas Eve of 1967 was passing and nothing was left under the tree. After socks and underwear, flannel shirts and construction paper, my Christmas energy had fallen to the floor with the empty wrappings. Through a fog of disappointment I heard my aunt's voice,

"Scott, here's a box with your name on it."

I was too worn down to expect anything but more Avon products; maybe frog soap on a rope. I half-heartedly tore off the paper. The box claimed it was a radio, but experience had crushed my hopes before; old boxes often housed new unexciting gifts. But when I saw its modern plastic shape and the smell of electronics, I screamed,

"A radio! A transistor radio!"

Mom's face showed surprise. She wondered who gave me this unusually expensive gift. The tag said Grandpa. I guess he knew I needed access to the world. Now I could scan the AM dial and seek the sounds I liked.

Radio was a voice of daily life. Polka music blared from the dusty radio in Grandpa's barn during milking. WCCO was the soundtrack of my childhood. Mom kept it on morning through night: Joyce Lamont, Arthur Godfrey, the noon farm report with Maynard Speece, Boone and Erickson, Chuck Lillegren, Jurgen Nash, Howard Viken, and after nine, when I was lying in bed, Hobbes House.

But this was not my music. The Beatles were out there somewhere, The Rolling Stones, The Miracles, Dusty Springfield; snatches heard on car radios as fathers twisted through the dial in search of their music, not the music blasted by unruly teens swimming at the bridge or the rope swing.

Dad liked hangdog honky tonk, Mom despised it, so it was discouraged in the house unless his army buddy Ernie was visiting. Dad had free reign in the garage or downstairs in his darkroom, so it was Hank Williams and baseball, Paul Harvey and the opinions of other AM radio philosophers.

Hockey practice commenced in third grade. A radio played across the ice through a speaker hung on the warming house wall, a radio controlled by Leroy, the surly, unshaven, village maintenance man who plowed snow and picked up dead dogs in a dump truck. The collar of his grubby grey button-down union suit only became grubbier as the winter progressed. That AM radio, eternally tuned to KDWB, at the persistent demand of teenage girls, became my beacon.

Now late at night, like generations before, I explored the AM dial in the dark, seeking the exotic and unfamiliar, scraps of foreign languages, tuning into stations from Little Rock, Chicago, or Texas. They rose from the static and faded away in the middle of some great song. Fiddling with the dial never brought them back.

Later that year, Uncle Charlie gave me a ride home from Hanska; a hundred and twenty miles of me and him in his '63 Ford Falcon, two-door, hard-top, with the red bucket seats and the four on the floor. He let me choose the station, something no one had ever done. I searched the dial for rock and roll, found the Monkees and left it there. Next, they played the "Magical Mystery Tour."

Charlie asked if I liked "Acid Rock". I'd never heard of it, but figured he was talking about the music I'd chosen.

"Yeah," I replied.

He looked worried and changed the channel. Apparently, the music I liked was dangerous. I didn't know "Acid" was slang for LSD. For me, it brought corrosion to mind; that's what I liked, a musical equivalent of Drano. I pictured Batman and Robin being dunked into a vat of sulfuric acid by some criminal mastermind.

I'd always looked up to Charlie since he had a stereo console and a record collection of Motown he acquired in the Army. He was 27 years old and the epitome of cool. Now I had to question that.

In the middle of 4th grade, Mrs. Lorentsen announced that during lunch recess, we could bring records to play on the class phonograph. I wanted to participate, wanted to join the community of recorded music.

I had no older siblings, no hand-me-downs, no records except Mom and Dad's, which were obviously unacceptable; Oklahoma, Burl Ives, Mitch Miller. Most of my friends had older siblings and choices. Jackie Lundeen brought his brother's copy of *In-A-Gadda-Da-Vida*. Jesse Jenkins brought in two of his sister's 45s, The Rolling Stones "Paint it Black" and "Play with Fire".

Those two songs had an intoxicating texture that changed my life, I wanted to live inside them. As I stood beside the phonograph cart, I noticed that same look of concern on Mrs. Lorentsen's face.

I did own a record, but it wasn't something I could imagine bringing to school. It wasn't even really a record. It came embossed on the back panel of a box of Alphabits cereal, and you cut it out on the dotted lines when the box was empty.

I told Mom I needed a record to bring to school. "Isn't there something around the house you could use?" she asked.

"It can't be just any record," I replied, "It's supposed to be a record of music you like." And Mom said, "Well why don't you bring your paper Archies record?"

After a meltdown I was promised a 45 of my choice, from Hit Tunes Records and Refrigeration in Anoka. Unfortunately, my best friend Sweazy was present, and the paper Archies reference got around and dogged me on the playground for years to come.

"Hey Scott...Where's your paper Archies record?"

I'd flipped through the racks at Hit Tunes Records before, but this time I had the dollar and three cents in my pocket that allowed me to leave with two songs of my choice.

But which two?

It would definitely be the Beatles, ever since I was crowned with that Beatle wig by one of Dad's friends. I finally selected "Hello Goodbye" because I'd heard it on their recent Ed Sullivan appearance. The flip side was "I am the Walrus".

When I got home, and put it on Dad's stereo, "Hello Goodbye" played as expected: cascading pop harmonies. When I flipped to "I Am the Walrus", it sounded like it was on the wrong speed. There was no melody, no pop hook, and it wasn't really about love.

Soon I liked it better than the A side. "Sitting on a cornflake" and "yellow matter custard dripping from a dead dog's eye," were images I could understand, a visual landscape. Just follow the lyric instructions: "Elementary penguin singing Hari Krishna, man you should have seen them kicking Edgar Allen Poe," and who were these Eggmen descending into that apocalyptic surge that obliterated all?

John Lennon's theory of perfect pop song length was two minutes and fifty seconds. By the time I set the needle down on "Hello Goodbye" and got back on the couch, it was half over. "I Am the Walrus" changed time's shape, and in the world of the single, at 4 minutes and thirty-three seconds, it was virtually symphonic.

The next day, I handed Mrs. Lorentsen my record. I wanted to play "I am the Walrus", but felt afraid, knowing that "Snoopy vs. the Red Baron" was a class favorite. If a lot of kids brought records, she might play only one side each. I left it to chance and sat at my desk.

"Hello Goodbye" played and passed without notice, then Mrs. Lorentsen announced who brought it and flipped to the B side. I couldn't believe it was happening. Thirty seconds into the song everybody was looking at me, it was beyond liking or disliking, it was, "Where are you taking us?" From that moment forward, I was nicknamed Walrus.

Secretly it made me happy.

The Fifth Horseman

In the Beatles' era, four common names became iconic. The Bible had a couple books named after them. Even my dad shared one: George. But he wouldn't use it. It wasn't a name he liked. It sounded too old-fashioned to him. I couldn't understand it. He had one of the names of the four horsemen of the apocalypse and he wouldn't use it?

Nobody got Ringo's name, so it was down to 3 possibilities. I would have been happy with even a middle name, but my middle name was the same as Dad's middle name, the one he rearranged into his first. Everyone called him Eddy. I didn't want to be Eddy. The only other Eddy I knew was Eddy Munster, with the vampire cowlick. Why couldn't dad's middle name be George? Then my middle name would be George, and I could rearrange it into my first and live in the world of having my name be a Beatles' name, like those Catholic boys in school.

Not everyone knew dad as "Ed". Grandma called him Eddy because she always did what made him happy. Grandpa continued to call him "George". Grandpa was traditional, a name was given to you at birth and you lived with it. There were better things to do than worry about names. Hell, there was work to get done. His own father's name was Ignatius, for god's sake, and you never heard him complain.

The only other people who called him "George" were people from his childhood who hadn't heard he reinvented himself. Whenever I answered the phone and heard the heavily-accented Minnesota dialect ask for George, I knew which part of his life they were calling from.

Dad's favorite movie from his youth was *God Is My Co-Pilot*, based on a novel by a guy named Colonel Robert Scott. This saved me from my mother's dream of calling me Benjamin James. I became Scott Edward.

In that era of revolutionary music, I never found a rock star to elevate my name. I had to go it alone.

Instructions

My grandfather had a faded circle worn in the back right pocket of his jeans. It was where he slipped his round cardboard can of chewing tobacco. If I was around when he switched over, I got the empty one.

He used them for screws, or the little white grubs he harvested from goldenrod galls, packed with cornmeal, and stacked in the freezer for ice fishing. All I did with mine was twist off the metal lid, and sniff the fragrance; like sweet leather or whiskey, then slide it back on to keep the smell inside.

Grandma called it a dirty habit, not something you wanted to cultivate, but how a man conducted that habit was how she judged his merits.

Anyone who carried a jar inside the house to dribble his snoose into was a weasel; real men walked outside to spit.

These were matters of etiquette; not distinctions I understood as a man with the chaw in his cheek, until that day in the barn, when I was ten. Grandpa paused for a pinch, saw me watching, and held out that open can black as coffee grounds.

I'm not sure why he offered. His only instruction was "Don't swallow it," as I packed the snuff against my gum. I remembered him telling once, how his brother Fritz got sick on their old man's tobacco when they were kids. If this was cautionary, it was sink or swim.

Within moments his warning was washed away. The levee that held my saliva back was breached, snuff loose, water rising.

I held onto a post, bent over, opened my mouth and let it drool onto the straw. Grandpa waited. When I raised my head, wiping my mouth on my sleeve, all he said was,

"Don't tell your grandmother."

The Great Leap Forward

Summertime in the 1960s. Moms were home, kids ran wild. We left in the morning, came back for lunch, for chores, for supper, and when it was too dark for kick the can, maybe a bath, and then to bed.

The Lofton's lived in the woods and chipmunks had run amok. The cute little rodents were everywhere, undermining sidewalks, stealing dog-food from the garage, and all manner of terrible things.

Sweazy's dad engineered a cure; harnessing our *Lord of the Flies* energy for a campaign, he promised, would make the world a better place.

The little chipmunks had been our friends, for years we coaxed them to eat from our hands, attempting to speak their language, and now suddenly, without earning even a bounty for our treachery, we became foot soldiers in a declared war.

We were sent out with a saw and instructed to cut a sapling the size of a walking stick. Light enough to be quick, long enough to have reach, and when swung, enough heft to cause damage.

The approach was primitive, similar to Chairman Mao's smash sparrows campaign during the Great Leap Forward.

Sweazy's older brother and his friends christened them beater sticks, carving notches into them like fighter aces did.

Chasing the chipmunks down, we merged into a stick swinging troupe of bloodthirsty apes, but when that tiny striped squirrel hugged the backside of a tree, cute as a cartoon, all the banshee yelling in the world didn't make it easier to swing like Harmon Killebrew and splatter it like a fly.

Crushing your first chipmunk was tough.

We learned to wield our sticks with finesse, more like a shotgun than a howitzer. We learned to forget our childhood's allegiances. We learned to take sides. We learned that defending territory was a painful exercise.

Dad's Lesson

I was nine and having trouble selling my Scout-O-Rama tickets. It wasn't altruism that drove me. It was that pamphlet of prizes you could win for selling them. I was focused on a pair of swim-fins, mine for the sale of a mere twenty tickets.

Like the Kirby and Fuller Brush-men before me, I chose the door-to-door route. The cold call. Forgoing time-honored pitches, I opted for an informal approach, more streamlined, more suited to my style,

"You don't want to buy a Scout-O-Rama ticket, do you?"

I walked the roads and side-streets, the carpeted hallways of apartment buildings, through the suppertime jumble of cooking smells. I walked the River Road, the River Terrace, rang doorbells and knocked on windows, I was getting nowhere. I mean who really wanted to go to Scout-O-Rama? A lady with white carpet and a poodle bought one, some sad-eyed Jesus-haired man who didn't look like he was from around here bought one, my mom bought one, my grandma bought one. It was two days from the deadline, and I was nowhere near those blue-rubber swim-fins.

Dad had an idea. After supper we drove down to the American Legion. I climbed up on a stool. Dad ordered a beer and bought me a coke.

It was about seven o'clock and all these guys had been on the same stools since they got off work. It was a horseshoe bar where you faced people across the aisle and dad told them I was having trouble selling tickets for the Scout-O-Rama.

They sat there, half-drunk with their cash on the bar. Maybe they should have been home with their families. Maybe their kids were grown and moved on. Maybe they had nowhere else to go. So I walked around to each stool and laid a blue ticket on the bar. It was a bargain. For the price of a Whiskey-Seven they could redeem themselves and gain entrance to scouting's annual pageant of camp-craft. Some got teary-eyed, some even bought two tickets. That night, they purchased their dignity, and I earned my swim-fins.

The Camping Craze

In the sixties Coleman was the Chevrolet of camping. Stores sold the concept like an automobile showroom, filled with rows of standing tents, coolers and lanterns, sleeping bags and cots. You could try out different campsites and pretend you were camping. Dad fell under its spell, but Mom couldn't understand why sleeping on the ground was fun, and what about the bears?

Dad bought a canoe in '67, we were Boundary Waters bound by '69.

Mom did some research and found distressing studies that linked the presence of menstrual blood to an increased level of bear attacks, which as a woman, she felt, put another target on her back.

If we had to camp anywhere, Mom wanted an island. It felt safer surrounded by water; moat against an army of marauding bears. But Dad pitched camp on a peninsula; appendix to the forest primeval. Our food was hoisted in a duffel-bag, beyond reach of the critters, tied high in a pine.

We four shared a tent, not one single graham cracker allowed inside. Mom and Dad stretched out against adjacent walls, heads meeting in the corner. My sister and I slept between them.

Campsites attract visitors, skunks and raccoons mostly, scavenging in the night.

Mom expected the worst and Dad was already snoring away, hands flung above his head, fingers reaching. She was still awake hours later, listening to each rustle and squeak beyond the canvas, picturing a family of hungry bears, their sharp claws, the thinness of the tent's protection.

Dad stretched his arm out, hand grazing mom's hair. He could sleep through a tornado, but woke up quick when Mom hissed, "Bear!"

"Where?" Dad asked, his fingers clenching.

"There." Mom replied, her voice even more strangled.

"Where?" Dad croaked.

"Hair." Mom said, "My hair!"

The Night the Revolution Came Home

It was a little after midnight. I awoke to a different music than Dad was playing when I fell asleep. It had gone from the Ventures to "The Ballad of John and Yoko".

I sat at the top of the stairs and listened to the party in full swing, then I went downstairs and walked over to the stereo. Stacked on top was a pile of albums other people had brought.

The world was changing. The younger guys at the studio were a generation inspired by Bob Dylan, not the New Christy Minstrels.

Dad's music had been collected over previous decades, recorded onto flat boxes of Scotch brand reel to reel tapes, but at the eleventh hour, his doubts howled with such intensity that we drove to Shopper City to find something new. I showed him what was cool, what records he should buy, but when Dad saw what an LP was going for, he headed for the discount bins.

We returned home with a stack of Ventures and Herb Alpert recordings. He knew he was wrong, but he pushed through his feelings, like always.

The next morning when I got up, the house was silent and smoky, the stack of records still there, forgotten, or like magic, maybe someone sensed what I needed. Flipping through I found it, the latest Beatles album. I held it against my nose, inhaled its record store smell.

I'd been listening to the Beatles all my life. I tried to stay awake the night they were on Ed Sullivan but fell asleep. They started out with matching suits but wizened with each successive album; mustached and Jesus-haired, wearied by the weight of the world. I followed each incarnation. They were apostles and each 45 felt like an answer.

I walked through the party wreckage, eating whatever food was left from mostly empty bowls, sniffing forgotten drinks, lipstick-smudged cigarette filters afloat in dark liquids.

Mom and Dad woke up later, they were arguing. Mom was mad. She didn't like Dad's work friends. They were disrespectful and smoked funny cigarettes, people were making out with people they weren't married to.

I imagined Mrs. Fetterman, our neighbor, who worked at the lumber yard, squeezed behind a card table in the corner, French-kissing the paisley-ascotted Shane. Funny, Dad's work friends never had last names.

Tilt-A-Whirl

I called Poinzy to tell him someone forgot the new Beatles album at my house and he came over to listen, like some outstanding treasure washed up on our shore.

We sat downstairs in that empty room, listening, 'til the needle hit the end of the groove and I had to flip it.

Upstairs, Mom imagined key parties beckoning from the bottoms of emptied punchbowls. In London, the Beatles were imploding and I hoped they weren't really breaking up. In bed with the lights off that night, I listened to my transistor radio with the single earbud, holding out hope. On TV, the world was on fire, and Doris Day's face was still out of focus.

Ghosts

Sweazy and I were in 6th grade, not too old for candy, but bored with Trick or Treating. That rubber band around the neck bed-sheet Georgie the Ghost costume wasn't gonna do it anymore, but growing up in the Halloween Capital of the World made it unthinkable to give up.

I'd graduated to soaping windows and toilet papering trees the year before. I didn't feel like dressing up, but how about dressing our younger siblings in something we'd never wear ourselves? That was prank worthy. We created the outrage; they walked it to the door.

Halloween was supposed to be scary, but I couldn't find much to fear in werewolves and vampires. We wanted more. Born into the victory parade of the Good War, what was scarier than the ultimate evil of our century: Adolf Hitler.

When it came to scary, the Nazis knew what they were doing; well-tailored, dark uniforms framed with black leather, lightning bolts, and death's head skulls. Birds of prey and twisted black crosses displayed on blood red fields. Lines of torches burning in the night. They had a detachment of partisans called Werewolves: after-hours assassins dressed as civilians by day.

The German novelist Gunther Grass said he joined the Waffen SS at 16 because it looked cool. His father was a grocer and against the war. What teenage boy wants to run a grocery store. Sure, the good guys were good, but these bad guys looked so cool. Stylistically, the Americans were a working-class army, a bunch of guys in green dungarees and baggy jumpsuits. Heroes of destruction, not angels of death.

At first Perry and Nora were happy to be the subject of our focus. Nora was eight and Perry was ten. We dug around in our parents' closets and found what we needed: a white shirt, a skinny black tie, a wide leather belt, a black trench coat, and the biggest score of all, khaki riding breaches and a pair of knee-high leather hunting boots Sweazy's grandmother wore in the '20s.

The clothes fit Perry perfectly, so we cut and pasted a swastika armband from construction paper, greased his black hair down over his forehead, magic-markered a little Charlie Chaplin mustache beneath his nose, and from the toy box, put a replica Luger in his hand.

We dressed Nora up in military surplus fatigues and Dad's old army boots, pulled a rubber skull mask over her head, and crowned it with a WWII civil defense helmet. She wondered what she was supposed to be, and we told her, Dogface, ghost of an American G.I.

Then we marched them into the kitchen to show Mom. Perry gave a little heel click like on *Hogan's Heroes*, a Nazi salute, and a Teutonic "Trick or treat!"

"That's terrible." Mom said, barely suppressing a laugh, like she always did, when we premiered another assault on good taste.

At dark we unleashed our campaign on the neighborhood. Sweazy and I hid in the bushes around the corner of each house, where we could watch and listen.

Lugar drawn, Perry pounded on each door with his gloved fist, shouting "Trick or treat." Nora slouched along silently, vision obscured, sweating beneath her rubber mask, shambling in her oversized boots.

There were slamming doors and "You should be ashamed of yourselves". I don't remember what we expected, but the treats they got were begrudged.

This wasn't like egging houses or soaping windows where the fun was imagining their anger. But now we saw it. We imagined it would be like Candid Camera, that hearing it would be the pay-off. We didn't understand we had the power to raise the dead.

At the last house an older woman with a European accent answered the door.

"You terrible children!" she cried, "I came to this country to get away from this! I never thought it would follow me here, to my door."

Military Industrial Complex

After checking out Mao Tse-Tung's book on guerilla warfare from the Champlin library, I realized the advantage a home team had defending their land against invaders unfamiliar with the terrain. Sweazy and I decided new fortifications were in order.

We dug a slot trench in the woods to repel any designs on neighborhood conquest. We grubbed it out chest deep, tore a rusty old fence down for the barbed wire and strung it around the perimeter. We pulled over tall saplings with ropes and staked them to the ground for camouflage.

For a while we hunkered down in our bunker and scanned the horizon for hostile forces, but none appeared. It was the height of the Cold War, there was no action.

Civil Defense loses vitality without an enemy. To keep the narrative going we had to find one, an opponent that inspired us to greater heights of paranoia. The

Soviets were drab and overplayed, we were tired of the nuclear threat; we wanted old-fashioned hand to hand combat.

Two-hundred and fifty miles to the north stretched an international border with Canada. The Canadians were close, which itself was a threat. If they invaded no one would expect it, but if they dared, we would be ready.

All we needed now was a label to slur them with. Everybody hated communists, so we melded the two concepts and christened them Communist Canadians.

We started training, recruited Perry, Beej, Denny, and Brent. We collected bows, arrows, pellet rifles and bb guns. We liberated a white linen laundry bag from Mom, and I magic-markered a caricature of our neighbor Mr. Jankowski on one side. We filled it with straw and hung it from a pulley to slide across some clothesline strung between two big trees. When the target was towed uphill and let loose, we opened fire.

Mr. Jankowski purchased Sweazy's grandparents place after they died. It lay directly between my house and Sweazy's. Jankowski was an old polish guy with a strong accent who owned a bar down the road and drove a turquoise Studebaker with fins. The size of our territory had been reduced by his purchase, partitioned off like Prussia.

We claimed an unspoken easement, retaining our historical rite of passage between Sweazy's house and mine. Mr. Jankowski never complained, never wronged us, he even let kids play foosball in the bar, but when you start creating enemies, the list grows fast.

Sweazy's dad was an outdoorsman, happy to see us practicing archery skills on a moving target. On closer inspection he was dismayed to see our target was the effigy of a human, not a deer. He was even more alarmed to see the name of our neighbor scrawled beneath it. We told him we were in training to repel an invasion of Communist Canadians.

Our ignorance appalled him. His own father had volunteered for the Canadian army and fought with Canada in the Great War. "Stop calling them communists!" he shouted, "They're not communists, they're just like us."

We'd been raised with gun safety, a responsible handling of firearms. It was ingrained in us to treat all guns as loaded and never point them at anyone. But with this escalation, we began making exceptions. We decided the pursuit of realism was a priority. In basic training, live ammunition is fired over the heads of G.I.'s as they crawl beneath barbed wire. To become men, we would have to set aside our mother's warnings.

We decided it would be cool if someone hid behind a tree and someone else blasted the bark off over their head, just for effect. We agreed on two rules: three pumps max, no shots at people.

But five pumps tore the bark off trees a heckuva lot better than three, and if effect was the point of breaking rules, then why not break another for the greater good?

Crawling around, taking shots from behind trees and embankments, I spied Brent's bare elbow sticking out from behind the trunk of a cottonwood. I lined up my sights on it just to see what it felt like. It felt good, so good I couldn't stop myself and pulled the trigger.

There was a pause and Brent rolled out in a fetal posture, gripping his elbow. He called me a son of a bitch. I apologized, explained the esthetics, but it was his arm, and I was a fucking asshole.

We kept playing, but now the game was colored by vengeance. We no longer had a treaty; no rules, just emotion. Brent carried the bb pistol my dad bought to scare off the marauding neighborhood dogs that knocked over our garbage cans. It didn't have the range of a pellet gun and couldn't kick any bark off a tree. Lulled into complacency, I expended a beautiful shot in a truly artistic manner, knocking into motion a movie perfect spray of debris.

Suddenly, pistol raised, Brent was up and running toward me in some crazed Banzai charge as I fumbled with my unloaded gun. He knew I had nothing to threaten him with; no round in the chamber, no moral high ground. He pulled the trigger point blank and hit me right in the middle of the forehead. It stung. My eyes watered but were still intact. There was no way to retaliate, my only option was, be a man and grimace.

Beyond our neighborhood, the communists were winning. I was thirteen and Nixon had just ended the draft, calling it Peace with Honor. Mom was relieved; I was off the hook. She always insisted, if the war was still going when I turned eighteen, I should move to Canada.

Cat in the Sack

It was Sweazy, Phil Lund, and me. Whether it was chewing gum or talking in class, we did so much of it that Mr. Olson assigned us sentences due the following morning, to be written on notebook paper 200 times:

"I will not talk in class."

Maybe there was something good on TV or maybe it was just really nice out, but the next day no one had those sentences done.

So, Mr. Olson doubled it, due the next day, and we didn't get it done either.

By the end of the week, we turned in what we had each morning, like some phony currency, falling deeper into debt each day.

Every night after supper, we became human sentence factories. At the kitchen table, television blaring from the other room, we cranked out product, writing words thoughtlessly down the page like a ledger:

I I I will will will not not not talk talk talk in class class class.

One morning Sweazy was up to 1600 and turned in 300 from the night before. When that doubled, it was 3200 and everyone in class started laughing as he stood beside Mr. Olson's desk. All he could do was laugh too.

Halfway around the world in Vietnam, boys six years our senior were filing sandbags by the hundred for equivalent infractions.

It wasn't working there either.

Going for a Can of Coke

Twelve years old, peering out from behind my hair. Hockey coach yelling, "Vetsch, get that hair outta yer eyes!"

Summer now, neighborhood windows aglow at twilight with the canned laughter and drone of evening TV.

Like a salmon drawn upstream, I felt the pull of a social world that didn't exist, not in the classroom ruled by teachers, or the raucous limits of a boy scout meeting. A fort in the woods with your buddies didn't solve it either.

Nowhere for a kid to go, no bargains in a world of adults. Nothing at Keno's Pizza, the Legion Club, or the River Inn. The grocery store closed at nine, nothing but roaming the streets.

A can of coke was a reason to walk, a physical destination. There was a pop machine outside the locked door at the Sinclair station. In that empty lot beneath the green dinosaur, moths fluttered about the lit-up pop machine. Streetlights buzzed.

It wasn't about hanging with friends or watching TV, it was about pursuing a solitary course, calibrating your soul's compass.

Certain nights I crossed paths with a girl I recognized from school. We'd say hi and keep walking, her bell-bottoms dragging ragged in the gravel.

She awakened the emptiness; walking was a cure.

Fun Facts Club

In fourth grade we knew where babies came from. We watched bulls mount heifers, drakes on hens, dogs humping your leg with their lipstick out. We were pretty solid on the how, still working on why.

Adults conspired to keep us in the dark, so we formed the Fun Facts Club. Meetings were held weekly to present the data we gathered. TV, magazines, movies, and books were combed for clues, jokes deconstructed. Why was that funny? What was a rubber? Why did teenage boys keep them in their wallets?

Jackie had a brother in high school, who kept his condoms in his sock drawer. Jackie swiped one, opened the foil, and said it looked like a brown balloon.

I was scribe, so I drew his description for the archives. I based it on the rubber thing Mrs. Lorentson wore on her index finger when she graded papers, not a bad likeness except it was thicker and perforated with small holes. I added the holes to my drawing, clearly misunderstanding the fundamentals.

Our first meeting was after school in Burton Cosgrove's basement, an idea inspired by *The Flintstone's* Loyal Order of the Water Buffalo.

Dennis Mayer brought the gavel, and being ten years old, we all carried proxies of ourselves. The laundry detergent Bizz had shrink-wrapped plastic figurines from the Pogo comic strip onto bottles of liquid detergent. Everyone had one, even me, and my mom only used powdered.

We sat on the floor around the circular construction paper meeting house glued together in art class. We cut out a door for each Pogo character to walk through onto the meeting floor. The gavel tapped us to order, and Churchy LaFemme, Albert the Alligator, Porky Pine, and Pogo himself, entered from their respective doors and faced each other.

We couldn't figure out why people did it. We asked Mrs. Lorentsen if we could stay inside and have our club meeting instead of going out to the playground after lunch. She asked, "What kind of club is it?" We laughed, and replied in unison, "The Fun Facts Club."

"What kind of facts are you discussing?" She wondered, and asked to sit in.

We pulled up chairs around her desk while she ate, avoiding the topic that drew us together, while to our surprise and her relief, we discussed equally fascinating topics; Pink Panther, Bugs Bunny, and who was cooler. And to impress her, we dug out all our facts about tadpoles.

Once the facts were exhausted, we were in the wilderness. No one could explain why beds pushed down the street on *Love American Style* were funny, or help us surf the innuendo of *Laugh-In*. We backslid into *Rat Patrol* and *F-Troop*, built models. We fell in heartbreaking love on the playground; notes passed from desk to desk, glances encouraged or rebuffed. Do you like me? Mark the correct box with an X. Yes, no, or maybe.

But the question of why people had sex still remained. The answer emerged when I had forgotten there was a question.

It was a Monday evening, deep winter, already dark. I walked to Sweazy's house, wearing my hockey equipment, stick and skates across my shoulder. We were in 6th grade and his mom was driving us to practice. She was washing dishes, said Sweazy was in his room.

I slipped off my boots and headed down the hallway. Sweazy weirdly shut the door behind me. I sat on the edge of his bed. Something that looked like an electric razor was plugged in on his pillow.

Sweazy said he pulled a muscle in his leg the week before and his mom gave him that electric massager to use on it. Cindy, his ninth-grade cousin, had been there on Sunday afternoon for some family thing, saw it on his bed and laughed.

"Do you know what you can do with that thing?" she scoffed, like it was a bomb. Then she told him.

"If you put this on your dick," Sweazy said, parroting Cindy, "It feels really good."

It was like he asked if I wanted a graham cracker or something, I mean how good could it feel?

He told me to try, he'd watch the door.

In less than a minute Moses was coming down the mountain. In that moment I noticed the ring of pubic hair, like I'd been in a time warp, like I hadn't really seen my body in a long time. It was like discovering the atom bomb; something huge no one bothered to mention.

With mushroom clouds rising in our eyes, we sauntered back through the kitchen, grabbing skates and sticks, and climbed into their station wagon.

In the following days, all programing was preempted. We took turns. One person stood guard watching for his mom, the other did the deed. In school we told our friends and word swept like a grass fire.

Denny Bittner got back to me the next day; turns out you didn't need the massager, you could do it with your hand. He said he figured it out sitting on the toilet. That night, I locked myself in the bathroom. Denny was right, but the massager was better. Sweazy's little brother proved it worked on fourth graders too, told us he peed a couple drops.

It became known as "The Buzzer." Derek Lamprey, who had yet to grasp the gravity of the situation, called it "Bizzy Buzz Buzz," after a toy advertised incessantly on TV. We wondered if Sweazy's mom understood what you could do with this thing. The directions on the box were cryptic. Why was it on a shelf in their bedroom closet?

A few weeks later, Sweazy's mom decided his leg was healed enough, and took her massager back.

We were leaning on it pretty heavy by then and it was cold turkey. In desperation, Sweazy swiped it back, put the empty box on the shelf, and hoped his mom wouldn't need it. He snuck it over to my house, and the web of life continued. The brilliant part was now I could use it whenever I wanted.

I had an electrical outlet behind my bed and kept it plugged in on the floor, ready at a moment's notice.

My room was at the end of the house, just past the bathroom. I reached behind my bed, hauled it up by the cord, and flipped the switch. I could hear Johnny Carson's monologue from the living room.

Then I heard Mom coming down the hallway and snapped it off. She stood outside my closed door a few moments, then went back to the living room.

I switched it back on, heard Mom coming, flipped it off again and waited in silence. She knocked on my door, opened it enough to stick her head through.

"There's an electrical disturbance on the TV screen," she said, "Like something's running. Do you hear it?"

"No..." I replied, shaking my head.

"It sounds like it's coming from down here." she said, shutting the door.

With disappointment, I lowered it under the bed.

The next day after school, I walked into my room. Mom sat on the mattress. In her hand was the massager, vibrating against her palm.

"What do you use this for?" she asked.

"Sore muscles." I replied.

"Where did you get this?"

"Sweazy gave it to me. It's his mom's."

"I don't think you need this..." she said, turning it off.

I remained quiet.

"Do you?"

"Probably not," I replied.

Mom wrapped it up in a brown paper lunch bag and set it on top of the refrigerator. I walked over to Sweazy's house, and told him what happened. How would we live without it? We lamented.

But hormones helped us realize, far from being out of our hands, we were suddenly freed from hiding it. If Mom went to the grocery store or got her hair done, down it came, and before she was home, back it went, scrunched into that brown paper bag, now a legitimate part of the kitchen landscape.

That brown paper, gripped and grasped countless times, became crumpled and crinkled. Over time all the handling left it soft as suede, smooth as oiled buckskin.

I can only imagine Mom's realization, seeing the lunch bag's transformation, like finding a mouse nest in a drawer and just shutting it again.

Every *Leave it to Beaver* kind of family sit-com had a dad sitting down with his son to have that talk. It never happened. No one talked about it. The closest thing I heard, was Sweazy's dad telling him, "One day you and I are gonna lock antlers," but that was really about something else.

Mom probably meant to talk to Sweazy's mom about the massager but found it uncomfortable and procrastinated. The drama of the softening sack made her tired, like the sound of squirrels scratching in the attic.

Wordlessly one day, while I was sitting at the kitchen table, she snatched it off the refrigerator, went out the door, and dropped it into the milk box on the back porch.

It was a hot potato and remained that way, exiled with the frisbees and jump ropes, until Sweazy's mom discovered it gone from her closet. Sweazy explained that he loaned it to me for an injury.

She wanted it back, and once again, in the fashion of the times, the massager was returned to its box, utilitarian as a razor, never to be mentioned again.

Tilt-A-Whirl

I knew by sixth grade that I would never be a fighter pilot. Carnival rides made me sick. I loved the heights but motion killed me. One ten minute ride at the regional airfield with my uncle, had me running for the toilet as soon as the plane's door opened.

I observed that girls loved carnival rides, and our class was celebrating the end of the year with a field trip to Como Park, in Saint Paul. I had a girlfriend named Molly Hall who wore cute little red and white "Coke is the Real Thing" hip-hugger bell-bottoms and wrote me notes about wanting to see what I looked like in the dark.

There would be no dark on that hot June day, but the restrictions of our seating chart would be lifted. In the notes Molly wrote me, I noticed an "i" had replaced "y" as the last letter of her name, the dot above the "i" morphing into a little round circle, sometimes even a heart. I wasn't exactly sure what this "in the dark" business was about; it sounded ominous.

Earlier that year, an afternoon over Christmas break, I sat behind Maggie Miles on a sled, and she let me hold her budding breasts all the way to the bottom of the hill. I could feel them, though her coat, through the palms of my mittened hands, and it was a bolt from heaven. I asked her if she wanted to do it again and she said yes. But by spring she dumped me for my best friend Rory and then there was Molli.

The rituals of love were becoming complex. A new subtlety was required, something called romance, what Mom called the paperback novels she read every night on the sofa when her housework was done.

Everybody liked rides. Boys loved the out-of-control; we built ramps to jump bikes, did flips off rope swings into the Mill Pond, stepped onto moving ice-flows for a ride downriver. But this was different, this was a controlled out-of-control, an illusion of daring, some knowingness that brought the girls together in whispers and giggles. If a boy and a girl did that together it meant something, all you needed was money to pay the fare and a stomach for it.

I pretended to love rides too, but my body poised to betray me. I couldn't tell Molli my secret and didn't want to think about what would happen if I didn't. My only hope was to steer her toward the slow boat rides and pray. If that failed, I'd have no choice but to throw myself in and let it rip. Showing faith, I spent the entire five dollars my mother gave me on tickets for the rides.

Tilt-A-Whirl

At the park we paired off, leaving the gaggle of boys behind. The uncoupled chased each other around like squirrels; the haves and the have nots.

The sun was rising, shade retreating. Maggie, Rory, Molli, me, and a few other girls, walked toward the rides. Molli saw the Tilt-A-Whirl and squealed. That's what she wanted, first thing.

We stood in line laughing, but it felt like waiting in the gym to get a measles/rubella inoculation. I wanted everything to move slower, wanted time to enjoy my nonchalance, but within moments they were buckling us in.

The Tilt-A-Whirl is a small car that spins on bearings round a tight little track set on slanted steel plates. These plates turn on a larger wheel that wobbles round a vertical axis with six other spinning cars. Once the attendant snaps the bar down across your lap you cannot leave your seat and a diesel engine starts the big wheel turning and each car spins in its own little circle. If he hears a lot of screams, the carny pulls the lever down further and amps those RPM's up. Molli was screaming and God I wished she'd kept it to herself.

We were thigh to thigh, but spinning so fast, I could see her sitting across from me and when the vomit left my mouth, I could see its shape like a vortex engulf her from collarbone to crotch.

We stumbled down the ramp together. She looked at me once, then down at the powder-blue midriff blouse she'd chosen to wear on this last day of school. She was drenched in the curdled milk and Wheaties I'd eaten for breakfast, and I was dry, untouched, like one of those tornado miracles where half the house is missing but the pictures are still on the wall.

Girls ran to the rescue from all directions, and she was quickly obscured by the throng. They glared at me in disbelief. I stood there alone, witness to my changing fortune, this pre-teen fall from grace: I'd gone from boy with a girlfriend to leper. Turning away with a collective strut of mortification, they vanished into a restroom.

I wandered into the afternoon, my pocket full of ride tickets and not a dime to spend. Some of the wad I traded, for a wax-paper cup of coke. Down by the kiddy rides, I noticed Donny Reidel, slumped over queasily on one of the slow boats that circled, rising and falling on gentle waves. I handed the operator my ticket and climbed onboard.

Wash Under Your Shorts, Boys

On that first morning of summer camp, Tenderfoot scouts waved goodbye to their mothers, climbed aboard the orange school bus and were upended into the world of men. In two weeks they would learn why it was a good idea to brush their teeth and wash their faces. The onset of puberty was a cold lake. While most cannonballed in, some clung to the dock.

Kent Sanderson was a clinger. It was my second year at camp, and I was pushing thirteen. The adults pronounced us tent-mates, which was a bummer. I wanted to tent with a buddy and Kent was just some kid.

I was supposed to mentor him but mostly hung out with my friends and Kent retreated into a solitary silence. By the time I crawled into my sleeping bag at night, the lump of him on his cot had already turned away, facing the canvas.

In that first week, even the leaders noticed Kent wasn't swimming. He sat by himself in the shade, wearing the sweatshirt and jeans he arrived in. One look at his filthy black fingernails and the problem was clear, Kent wasn't washing. The rest of us at least got wet. But Kent was a cat on the beach, dustier and grubbier with each passing day.

Every afternoon Mr. Lofton shouted above the splashing tangle of limbs, "Wash under your shorts boys!" We thought that was funny, but he was right.

The adults were worried: "Was Kent uncomfortable with his body? Was the food disagreeing with him?"

He was still wearing the same clothes he came in, pulling more layers over the top like the Michelin man.

Kent said everything was fine.

I didn't tell anyone about the candy under his cot. I'd camped out enough to know, even if you wanted a stash, it was stupid to keep it in your tent.

We used military surplus wall tents without floors, stitched from heavy canvas. Once the tent was set up, we spread a sheet of black poly across the ground. The sides were staked down and pulled tight, but it was still a point of intrusion for any nocturnal visitor bored with acorns, jonesing for a little caramel nougat.

Perhaps Kent was a picky eater, maybe candy kept him on an even keel. Probably his mother sent it along to help with his homesickness, and each night he crawled into his sleeping bag to gorge like a hibernating beast. I don't know what he had crammed in there, but I spied him more than once eating those sweet, sticky, orange slices dusted with granulated sugar.

By the end of the first week, the bottom half of his face was a grimy beard of filth, and a musky stench of the outhouse wafted in his wake.

One night I awoke in total darkness, Kent's snores were buzzing like a clarinet with a cracked reed. It was then I heard a faint crackling on plastic and an odor of skunk I hoped was coming from far away.

My ears stretched out like antennae, seeking a sonic image.

The tent walls were staked as tight as I could get them, but between the stakes anything with a nose could slip through like a kid sneaking into the circus. Why wouldn't a skunk seek the high octane promise of Kent's candy stash?

I listened, straining to see. Eventually I made out a white stripe dancing in the darkness, then others, and realized it was a foraging mother leading her family on a prospecting expedition, and Kent's pack was the honey hole.

There were the sounds of feet on plastic and the periodic flag of a skunk's puffy tail passing my cot, but most of the action was in Kent's pack, cellophane crackling as they dug through it.

The air was skunky, my ears filled with crinkling cellophane and the smacking of pointy omnivorous teeth, gum deep in orange slices.

I was afraid to slap at mosquitos or brush off the legions of Daddy Longlegs marching across my sleeping bag, hunting for food. The whole world was working, only Kent slept.

I was stiff, desperate to change my position, but didn't dare. I wanted Kent to suffer like I was suffering, but if he woke up and freaked out, the detonation would ship us back home to a tomato juice bath.

I had to pee and clenched every muscle I could, like a bull rider at the rodeo. My only salvation was the hope that Kent had eaten most of his candy already. The skunks would only surrender when everything was gone.

I held myself motionless, finger in the dike, hypnotized by the dancing stripes as darkness greyed into dawn. I could see Kent's profile, like a mountain range, his nose the highest peak and the mama skunk rising up on her hind legs, trailing the scent of sugar. It was Kent's face she smelled, the grubby sheen around his lips, each breath circulating the candied fog of his sugar encrusted teeth. She hopped up on his chest like a kitty, sniffing at his face.

I shut my eyes, awaiting the mushroom cloud. In another moment she would lick his chin with her raspy tongue. His eyes would pop open, observe her peering into his face. His hands inside his sleeping bag would push up in a panic and launch her toward the ceiling.

When I woke up it was light. I checked beneath both cots, scrambled outside to pee, then crawled back inside and poked Kent awake. I told him what he slept through. What an idiot he was. What he put me through. I had finally become a mentor.

The next day I saw him at the beach in his layers of shirts, and crusty jeans.

He was staring blankly at the lake, a scoutmaster at his elbow, speaking sternly. I couldn't hear what they said, but he was unlacing his boots like they were the only thing that held him together.

Then he waded in. White legs and bony shoulders slipping beneath the surface, joining the rest of humanity, already washing under their shorts.

Addressing Mister Bader

In elementary school, practicing the curlicues
of cursive penmanship,
we learned you could interchange Master for Mister
when addressing an elder.
At summer camp, in Mr. Bader's woodcarving merit badge class,
someone blurted that out and we realized
it wasn't really incorrect
to call mister Bader,
Master.

Viva Zapata

It was the early Seventies. We were having tacos for supper, so Mom pulled down our perennial bottle of Zapata hot sauce from the cupboard above the cereal. We didn't eat tacos much, so it sat up there for years.

This was the era of Hamburger Helper. Convenience and a pound of ground beef found their way to every counter. For the more adventurous, hard-shell tacos became a sensation. Besides home cooking, the only box options were TV Dinners or Totinos Frozen Pizza.

Zapata was the brand-name before it became Zantigo in 1976. Zapata's ad campaign was badass. Zantigo was safer, not named after an armed revolutionary. General Mills owned it and didn't get where it was by naming product lines after confrontational historical figures and Dad worked for General Mills and that's why it sat in our cupboard.

He photographed the bottle, and he got to keep it.

The cap was gunky and stuck to the glass because Mom didn't refrigerate condiments like mustard or ketchup. As I tried to unscrew it, a bubble grew out of gunk in the threads. The more I tried, the bigger the bubble got. When I poked it with my finger, the cap blew off and I got a face-full of taco sauce.

I ran to the sink and washed out my eyes. As I wiped my face with a dish towel, I looked up to see a ragged circle of red on the kitchen ceiling with the cap stuck in the middle like a Veterans Day poppy.

"That's incredible!" Dad pronounced, "Did you see that, Elaine...That is incredible."

Dad was astounded, but that was nothing new, he was astounded by all tragedies great or small.

And that's how it stayed for the next five months. Friends were amazed at first, then wondered why no one cleaned it off, a question I could never answer. We just got used to it. After a while I thought it was cool that Mom left it up there; what began as a blemish became a decoration. Over time the edges crusted, and the whole bloom darkened.

I don't know what it symbolized, but the feeling was, maybe Dad should. If Mom was waiting for him to ask, he didn't. He ignored the stain. Perhaps Mom viewed it as a miracle, a visible manifestation; like the Shroud of Turin, proof that the unspoken truths crowding the room really were there.

The Fetterman Switcheroo

In the early '70s, the neighborhood moms began getting jobs. It was a big change. There were kitchen table arguments, and "over my dead body" replies. television comedians had opinions and so did the clergy, Archie Bunker had a thing or two to say.

Approaching our teen years, the trade-off for someone being there to fry you a grilled-cheese sandwich, in contrast to the freedom of an empty house when you got home from school, had a lot going for it.

Ray and Roy's mom was the first, she was employed by the Rum River Lumber company, working in the office, returning to a job she had during high school.

It was a revolutionary and never before experienced act: an abandonment of hearth and home. Draconian rules were drawn up in advance. Neighborhood children were no longer allowed to enter their house when the parents were at work. Doors were to be locked upon entering after school, and the boys bound to remain inside until a parent returned.

We were outraged. We'd grown up going from house to house unfettered, going through each neighbor's cupboards seeking better treats than those found in your own home. Now it was like they'd dropped out of NATO, there was a lack of access and reciprocity. We considered it a referendum on our trustworthiness and felt slighted, but realistically our track record did not reflect well on us.

We'd been shown *The Lord of the Flies* back in elementary school. The cruelty and violence were meant to shock us, but it was really just another day on the playground.

I remember looking out the window over the kitchen sink, seeing the Fetterman's white stucco house so spotted with rotten tomatoes and cucumbers that it looked like a loaf of Wonder Bread, and realized the phone would ring at any moment. We just went crazy sometimes, like the afternoon behind the Legion. We started out breaking a few empty liquor bottles and soon smashed barrels of them on a pile of rocks until a neighbor drove down and shook us to our senses like mad dogs.

We knew everyone's houses like they were our own. All keys were hidden outside. Eventually everyone knew where each key was hidden.

Mom safety-pinned ours inside a rug perpetually hung on the clothesline. The Fetterman's rested on a ledge beneath a metal awning shading their picture window. The Lofton's was inside a carved coconut monkey in their breezeway closet.

One summer weekend, while I was at my grandparents and the Fettermans were gone to Aitken in their camper, Sweazy performed a touch of espionage beyond anything we had ever imagined. He told me about it after school the following Monday, to explain Ray and Roy's contention at the bus stop that morning.

Perhaps he'd been feeling abandoned, a little sorry for himself, wandering the neighborhood alone, bored with fishing, trying to avoid the chores his dad would find for him.

He told me he took the Fetterman's key and let himself into the quiet of their house. He wandered from room to room and went through the kitchen cupboards, where he discovered a carton of Pall Malls. He slid out a pack, tore off the cellophane and foil, tapped out a cigarette, sat down by the big ashtray on their coffee table and smoked it.

After he stubbed it out, he walked into the bedroom shared by Ray and Roy. They each had a chest of drawers, their sacred objects placed on top; football cards, a baseball signed by some Twins outfielder, a model car, a Lake Superior agate.

He went through the drawers just because they were there. There were few surprises. Our lives were all laid out in such close proximity, that if Sweazy hadn't already seen what was in them, he could have based it on his own. Bottom drawers contained pants, middle drawers pull-overs and T-shirts, upper drawers socks and underwear.

In that upper drawer, each brother kept his wallet, and that formed Sweazy's plan.

He took all the money from Ray's wallet, slipped it into Roy's, and shut the drawer. Then he got the cigarettes and the ashtray and carried them back to their bedroom.

He leaned back on Roy's bed, lit up another one and smoked it. He set the ashtray on Ray's dresser and butted it out. He tossed the pack and a book of matches into Roy's underwear drawer, made sure all the elements of his trap were set, locked himself out, replaced the key beneath the awning, and walked home.

Boyhood Distractions

I told anyone who'd listen, I'd give 'em ten bucks

to drop their cut-offs and wade waist deep around Hickey Lake:

the whole circumference, the entire shoreline,

they could even keep their tennies on.

This gambit was inspired by my knowledge of the alligator snapper.

There were lots of snapping turtles in Hickey Lake,

but no alligator snappers,

they inhabited the southern end of the Mississippi.

These turtles employed a unique method of catching their dinner.

They dug themselves into the muddy bottom and opened their mouths.

Their tongues were pink, resembling a worm when wriggling. If a fish ventured near enough to snatch at it, the snapper shut its jaws.

The Hickey Lake Snappers, possessed the

snapping jaws, but were short the wriggling tongue. In this northern version, all elements would be

in play.

The dare was rhetorical.

Loop-O-Plane

Dad was drifting through the exhibits at the County Fair;

wood-splitters, water softeners, and windup frogs,

but found himself drawn like a Junebug toward the midway lights.

A lot of people were standing around the Loop-O-Planes

and he stopped to see why.

Those diesels were really screaming he said,

cockpits ratcheting round like hammers,

no let up at the peak,

a vicious relentless arc.

Dad figured someone pissed the carny off

for him to keep it cranked up like that.

When the doors opened,

he said Sweazy and me

spilled out,

green as the Groovy Ghoulies.

I never even saw Dad there,

just snuck around back and

puked behind a trailer.

At least that carny saved me

from spending the five-dollar bill I had

tucked in my shirt pocket.

When I got home

that was gone too,

shaken loose

like an apple from the tree.

The Great Escape

The last time J.P. and Rory slept over was a Friday night between sixth and seventh grade. Sleepovers had been organized around war movies on TV, but now we were watching *The Midnight Special* and J.P. wasn't into it. J.P. liked trains and we were building HO scale models. Rory was more interested in firecrackers and blowing up his childhood.

J.P. and Rory both loved Steve McQueen in *The Great Escape*; surviving the cooler by bouncing that baseball, doing what had to be done, stealing that motorcycle, trying to cross the border.

J.P.'s older brother and his friends were digging some kind of hide-out in a storm sewer under the street, at the end of their driveway. Each night they snuck out of their houses and climbed down the manhole to dig, hauling up buckets like Steve McQueen. They were smoking joints down there, drinking Boone's Farm Strawberry Hill.

Rory lived across the ball field from J.P. and became one of the diggers. J.P. hated the whole thing. I was a mile away, a long walk after curfew, plus Mom sat up half the night smoking cigarettes and reading romance novels on the sofa, she was hard to get around. Before I figured out how, they all got caught.

A crucial detail from *The Great Escape* had been overlooked: soil composition.

They were dumping their buckets on the driveway, raking it into the gravel, just like in the movie. But J.P.'s dad was smarter than the Nazis and it didn't take long before he wondered where all that sand was coming from.

After *The Midnight Special* we sat there, cross-legged, sleeping bags stretched out under the ping-pong table. We were looking at guitars in the Sears and Roebuck catalog. Rory pulled a pack of Winchesters out of his jean jacket pocket and offered me one. I took it, lit a match and pulled the smoke into my mouth, like every cool guy I'd ever seen on television.

J.P. rolled his eyes and dragged his sleeping bag across the room. Crawling inside, he pulled it over his head and turned his back on us. It was J.P. who jumped the fence. He made his great escape.

Sharp Tits

When I was a kid, all the women had sharp tits. Pages and pages of the Sears and Roebuck catalog showed women in Playtex bras, white and peaked as the snow-topped mountains. When bra styles changed, we realized everyone was different, and the world became a better place.

Barbies didn't have nipples, no one had nipples, just that pointy shape. My mother's bras, hung up to dry in the bathroom; their thick embroidered, grape-vine motif grasping a rigid foam cup, were designed like armor.

Breasts weren't utilitarian, they were a national treasure and needed protection.

Mom didn't wanna give me a Freudian Complex. She heard it all began with poop and boobs. It was safer to nurse me on cow's milk, warmed up in a glass bottle.

On the other hand, Mom didn't believe in depriving a pet of its sexuality, so our Siamese cat, Keeto, was never spayed and yowled one week out of four.

Keeto was our introduction to a very public display of female desire. Eyes glassed over, rear-end rising in the air, she pumped her feet rhythmically, tail twisting to the side to reveal her swollen vulva shedding a single tear like that sparkling drop of Retsyn, in the Certs' TV ad.

My friends were fascinated by this exhibition of the feelings we felt unrelentingly. Keeto loved boys. We knew menstruation was a monthly event and wondered if girls ever went into heat. We mostly figured they didn't, but it was nice to imagine.

My sister was the only girl in the neighborhood, so when a family moved in next door with two teenage daughters, my friends and I were ecstatic. We were in sixth grade, Karin was in eighth, Joyce, ninth.

After football practice one evening, still wearing our equipment, Sweazy and I ran around the front yard, throwing a ball, trying to look athletic. That was how we introduced ourselves, not impressive to junior high girls, but all we had.

Proximity put me in a great position. I could walk home with them after school and exhibit my cultivated maturity, sit at their kitchen table and smoke their mom's Old Golds. This worked great until Sweazy or someone else showed up looking for me with that lower lifeform boy energy; maybe dumping a glass of water on my head or blurting out a secret I'd shared in strict confidence, any act that dragged me down and fucked it up. I was trying to elevate the situation.

One afternoon Derek Lamprey showed up at my house: nickname "Leach". We were down in the basement, Keeto doing her dance. He picked up a pencil with a fresh pink eraser, touched it to his fingertip, and said, "Should I use this on her?"

I didn't want Derek around anymore, that was a big part of it. His squirreliness was something I wanted to leave behind. I couldn't help it if my friends weren't ready.

The next day at school I told everyone he tried to do it with my cat and his dick was the size of a pencil eraser. Derek retaliated by sitting behind Karin on the bus, telling her, I told everyone she let me feel her out.

He was telling the truth; I stupidly made that claim. Joyce and Karin were doing things like sitting on my lap, kissing me, and watching me blush. I wasn't lying but left out a lot of crucial context. At home Karin wore a red, white, and blue floral halter-top, cut from some slippery fabric, and her shape beneath it was something I pondered all summer; not really pointy, but ski jumpy.

Between AnnieAnnieOver, Kick the Can, and hanging out while she babysat her younger sisters, I was at their house nearly every day. On that August afternoon, she stood beside me in their garage, watching me write my name with my finger in the dust that covered a charcoal grill.

My hand moved slowly across the stamped metal, where it collided with her halter encased breast, my hand moved right, her breast held its ground. Our eyes never met, but fell with urgency on the point of collision.

The Day Brent's Brothers Jumped Off the Bridge

We were thirteen the summer Brent Hill ran over and said his brothers were gonna jump off the Mississippi bridge. The bridge was tall, river rocky and shallow except beneath that one arch the channel ran through.

Brent's brothers were village outlaws, on a first name basis with the local police. Their house was across a ditch from the elementary school. I never knew what their dad did for a living, but you could see him every afternoon on his porch in his undershirt reading the evening paper.

We raced down Dean Avenue, toward their house and caught up with them heading toward the bridge, rollicking after them like puppies.

They ignored us like we weren't even there, but it was a great day if they knew your name. They were fifteen and sixteen, already dropped out of school, not bad guys, just not good with rules.

Everyone knew the channel ran under the third arch, it was all rapids except for the channel, especially in late summer. It wasn't a bridge anyone swam off, if anything, it was a suicide bridge, so it had to happen fast, before anyone called the cops.

They hopped up on the parapet, shirtless in cutoffs. Wayne jumped first, arms spinning like propellers all the way down, Darrel was in the air before Wayne hit the water.

We leaned way over, watched them splash under, waiting for their heads to pop up, current sweeping them downstream toward The Point and the creek, half a mile down, then there was nothing left to do but walk home.

The First of Many Choices
Based On Love

For our entrance into seventh grade
we had to choose a language.
Our choices were Spanish, French, or German.
It was a question I knew the answer to.

My grandfather's first language was German.
Hogan's Heroes was my favorite TV show,
I could say raus, achtung, and strudel.
In the Sgt. Fury comics, words like schweinhund and blitzkrieg
filled the white bubbles that burbled from the mouths of
monocled Nazi psychopaths. They were my study guides.

Then I fell in love.

As Mr. Olson passed out the forms,
I sat at my desk,
eyes on Maggie Myles across the aisle in her purple Danskin

and cream-colored hip-hugger bell-bottoms.
I considered my allegiances to German and chose
   French.

Before 6th grade was a wrap, Maggie dumped me
   with a long and lawyerly note,
choosing my soul brother Rory who had already
   chosen German.

They didn't even make it through summer,
but in September there I was
slouched in French class like a silly child,
across the aisle from Maggie.

Practical students chose Spanish
because it was useful, you could use it
on this continent,

Maggie was college bound, an A student, French was
   an academic choice,
and running down the hallways were the *Hogan's
   Heroes* Crazies,
flaunting their choices,
hurling their guttural vocabulary at the world
   between classes.

.My consolation was Miss Beaumont,
the most knock-out teacher in all of Jackson Jr. High.
When the guys drooled I told them
she was the reason I chose French,
that I knew
that I planned it all along.

An Education

We were running through a cornfield above the creek
when I spotted a magazine between the rows,
face up in the furrow
like it fell from a plane.
I picked it up and it was golden.
Someone was coming out here to be alone,
counting back each row to return
and spend some time with his magazine.
During the Boy Scout Paper Drive,
we knocked on doors,
collected twined bundles of old
newspapers and magazines.
We were prospectors
for this kind of gold,

sorting through stacks of bags

and boxes in Ecklund's garage,

shouting out when a promising vein

broke through.

Penthouse and *Playboy* were

leafy and lush,

steeped in sunshine,

flush with carefully Coppertoned flesh;

but this corn porn was creepy.

Its models weren't tanned,

they looked like somebody's mom without clothes on.

Their skin had a blue florescent cast,

like they were standing naked in the mirror of

a gas station restroom:

not pretty,

not smiling,

not even pretending.

It totally begged for a chorus of jeering pubescent boys

reading the text out loud.

Grandma might say a soul's virginity was lost in the process, but we lived without it.

We recited testimonials to French Ticklers

bristling like catfish heads in our hands,

sang the blind praises of dildos;

chanting their holy names:

the Hammerhead,

the Double-dong,

the Destroyer:

Long and Hard

for the Daring.

On one long bus ride to Many Point Scout Camp,

we piled into a truck stop.

Waiting in long lines for the toilet gave us time

to scour the paperback racks for the raciest titles

and graphics.

Brent Hill swiped a copy of *Myra Breckinridge*:

her jack-booted, mini-skirted legs beckoned

from the cover.

It was written by a guy named Gore Vidal,

I'd heard his name before somewhere,

maybe on TV.

Turns out it was a primer to reactionary judges on the

Supreme Court

who ruled Vidal's last novel obscene.

It said so in the Forward, where we looked

to figure out why a penis was a Rehnquist and

anyone who had sex got Burgered.

Vidal replaced key profanities with the name of each justice,

and to instruct adolescent boys in political thought,

a mnemonic device is paramount.

That next summer, thanks again to the light fingers of Brent Hill,

our summer reading was *Once Is Not Enough*.

The title was promising, the cover art backed it up,

but after reading *Myra Breckinridge*,

we knew the difference,

Jacqueline Suzanne was no Gore Vidal.

Army Men

One morning in seventh grade, walking to my locker, I was greeted by the shocking rumor that I and my friends still played with army men. The threat was mortal, someone defected. I was too stunned to imagine who said it; all energy marshaled into damage control. I swung back with righteous disdain: "Army men? What in the hell are you talking about?"

The rumor was persistent, spreading like chicken pox. I insisted the story was bullshit, absurd, whoever was peddling it, out of his mind.

But who? I couldn't ask, it gave the claim credibility. I stonewalled, spent the day whacking it down wherever it rose: class, hallway, or lunchroom. By hockey practice that night I was gaining ground, and during the scrimmage, used the cold quiet to put some Perry Mason logic on it.

We did build models, had since third grade, and these models were military. Inside them or beside them, were the figures of men wearing, I had to admit, military uniforms, which in a loose definition did make them "army men". This was inconvenient and I cringed at the thought. I could righteously assert I did not play with them, it was more like a historical reenactment, but that difference would be lost on my accusers. Like our continued participation in Boy Scouts, the whole thing had to be hushed up.

But who broke ranks and why? It was self-incrimination, it was social suicide. I felt a malice in it. Who was least invested? Who had nothing to lose?

I hadn't noticed a cooling of passion in Sweazy or Poinzy, but Rory had begun blowing up his models with firecrackers on a sandbar down by the river, something I couldn't bring myself to do. I watched. He set up an amphibious invasion, dug the defending army into the sand, lit the firecrackers and walked away from it all.

Rory could hold an iron cross on the rings, something nobody else at our school could do. He'd grown a sparse mustache, could buy cigarettes at Tom Thumb, and was sneaking out at night to drink Boones Farm with Duane Campbell and Jesse Jenkins.

Even Poinzy noticed the lay of the land before I did. He never explained, but one day offered to sell me a coveted model of a Japanese battleship for half the purchase price. I jumped on it. Over the next couple weeks, he sold me more, but why was I buying them?

I wasn't building them, I wasn't painting them, I certainly wasn't playing with them.

Down in Poinzy's room one afternoon, feeling a strange lack of purpose, I asked him why he was selling his collection. He said he saw no future in models. He was divesting, saving the money I paid him to reinvest in stereo components.

I never bought another model.

Mechanics of the First Kiss

It felt terribly and hopelessly late, that by the fall of 8th grade, it hadn't happened yet. I was given opportunities but squandered each one in fear.

It was Friday night.

Sitting on the gymnasium floor at the junior high dance, our shoes piled up by the door, we watched a rock band play on the stage above the basketball court. Shelly Simonsen sat beside me, my arm around her back.

We should have been dancing, Shelly liked to dance, but that wasn't something I did, and it was too loud to talk. Leaning against the wall, side by side, I listened to the music with a singular focus. When I dared, I looked down at the side of her face, pressed against my shoulder, and she looked back at me, expectantly.

That was the moment you were supposed to kiss, I knew that.

Each time the moment rose, I let it pass, repeatedly, as if I had a grander vision.

I feigned an intense interest in the band, but as the clock ticked toward ten, my interior world devolved into a discord only Fellini could envision. I hoped somehow, as I experienced each increment of time, I would be pushed to reach across that un-trekked expanse and kiss her.

Shelly was losing patience; I knew that too. It was the second school dance this scenario played out, and I felt the pressure. When it was 9:45 and I had 15 minutes left to act, I knew it wouldn't happen, though I prayed it might, if I could only magically become someone else.

Facing the clock on the wall, I watched the second-hand advance. When the lights came on, Shelly stood up and left with her friends, bewildered. I walked outside to find my parents' car. When Mom asked, all chirpy, if I had fun, I nodded and threw myself into the back seat.

On Saturday night I heard the phone ring. Mom called out, "it's for you." I took it in the basement, waiting for her to hang up the kitchen extension. It was a girl, one of Shelly's friends, I didn't even know which one. "Why didn't you kiss Shelly at the dance?!" Mutely, I hung my head. "On Monday morning," she said, "you're going to kiss her, in the band practice rooms. Someone will be waiting at your locker." She hung up.

Sunday, I tried to distract myself, but was filled with dread. That night, and it wasn't the first time, I tried practicing with a pillow, but there was no point. It didn't answer the question of how to bridge the space.

Walking down the hallway on Monday morning felt like facing a firing squad. I considered avoiding my locker, but needed my math book.

I dialed the combination quickly, but as the door closed, there stood Edy Ingman, all five feet of her. "This way," she announced, and marched me through the throng, briskly.

I wasn't in band, never set foot in that end of the school. Edy led me into a short hallway of doors, opening into windowless, sound-proofed rooms, where students could blow their horns and bang their drums. It was dim, not many lights on yet. She pointed toward a door, leaned against the wall, and crossed her arms.

I turned the knob. The lights were off, but I could see Shelly's shape, her thick, kinky, parted in the middle, hair. As the door closed behind me, I found myself in darkness.

I faced her, twelve inches of space between us.

I wondered if she'd done this before and started talking; pointless, time-wasting talk. She never said a word, just put her arms around my neck, pulled me close, and kissed my lips.

"We did it!" I exclaimed, in a rush of relief, when she finally let me go. Then she kissed me again just to shut me up, but this time her tongue offered a revelation.

This was French kissing, I'd heard about that too but never knew why. It was physical. My head was swirling like I was gonna black out and everything suddenly made sense. I kissed her back. The fear was gone. I didn't wanna stop and I didn't wanna talk. It was like being dragged into a river, and when I pulled myself out, I was John the Baptist.

Smoking

I smoked because my parents smoked, even if I never wanted to do anything like they did.

My sister and I pleaded with them to stop, but not because we worried about their health. Riding in the backseat with them smoking in front was a terrible thing. I complained and Mom bought me Dramamine.

There was no awareness that respirating beings locked in a smoke-filled Ford Galaxy would feel distress. Distress was the view from the backseat, which if the concept existed, would be non-smoking.

When he wasn't sleeping, Dad smoked Pall Mall's. Mom was more discriminating; her smoking was a punctuation to each of Dad's cigarette sentences. I don't know if it was worse when both were smoking or whether it could get worse. I only knew that the first thing we did at the crackling of the lighter was crank open the tiny rear windows and stick our heads into the slipstream of the highway, which was only pleasant if you were a dog that enjoyed its flappy jowls whipping in the wind.

Any time it wasn't winter we begged them to open their windows. Dad loved his window open, elbow on the sill, fingers gripping the top of the door. The roaring surge diluted their smoke, but made it impossible to read a comic book. Mom had a hairdo to maintain, so the most you got out of her was a half window.

In the winter, if you snuck your window down a crack, Dad felt the cold draft snaking around his feet and asked who had it open. Then, sullenly and wordlessly, you cranked it shut.

In school, teachers encouraged us to talk to our parents about smoking. We made posters and signs in class that were supposed to guilt them into quitting.

Sweazy's parents were both non-smokers. They were like unicorns. It was claimed his father was allergic to smoke, but campfires didn't bother him. I wanted to say I was allergic too, but my resilience was proven.

It never occurred to my parents not to smoke inside the Lofton's house. They ashed into their virginal root beer-tinted glass ashtray, center-pieced like a stage prop on their coffee table; as commonplace in those days as a bar of soap on the kitchen sink. No one considered walking outside to smoke unless they wanted fresh air.

The Loftons opened all their windows after my parents walked home, curtains held the stale smell for days. It was a free country back then; air and water belonged to everyone. No one owned them. It was the Wild West.

When puberty injected my body with chemicals, smoking was suddenly something I wanted to do. For a junior high kid, compelled to wait on a bus-stop like a leashed dog, smoking was a visible choice.

Cigarettes were easy to pilfer at home, there was always a carton in the cupboard by the refrigerator, an open pack on the kitchen table, Mom never kept count.

Smoking wasn't like swimming; you didn't need lessons; you just had to look cool doing it.

I got off the bus one afternoon at the stop after mine, lit up and took a drag.

Some kid said, "You're not really inhaling."

"I am too."

"No, you're not...Watch..."

He said you had to suck it into your lungs right at the end of the drag. I did and it was like stepping off the Loop-O-Planes at the county fair.

"There you did it." he said.

Sweazy got hooked even though his dad was allergic. He just needed to wash his hands more and chew gum. His little brother Perry ended up smoking too 'cause he hung around with us.

Mom got her hair done on Friday afternoons, so everyone in the neighborhood knew, and the place was ours for a couple hours after school.

We were sitting on the back porch. Perry had just consumed a surprising number of plums. He ate them, dispassionately, one after the next, like a plum eating contest. When they were gone, he lit a smoke and just happened to really inhale for the first time. Soon he was on his hands and knees, puking up those plums on the lawn like a cat sick on grass.

It was a couple years before my parents discovered I smoked, long after I was buying Marlboros at Tom Thumb. Sweazy and I were ambushed sneaking a cigarette on a grey winter day, behind a car in the high school parking lot, and suspended for a week.

As usual, the next Saturday morning, Dad and I were in the garage, working on my grandfather's pickup. This was Dad's enforced labor program, designed to get me up in the morning and keep me off the street, avoiding his version of a misspent youth.

Dad was lighting his first cigarette of the day and offered me one. It was a coming-of-age moment, we lit up off the same match.

For one glorious week we smoked together, until a doctor's appointment revealed Dad had lost sixty percent of his lung capacity. I heard about it at supper. He didn't push back his chair and smoke his usual cigarette. He never smoked again.

It took another decade for mortality to find me wheezing away behind a hockey net during a neighborhood pick-up game. It was then I realized, if Dad could quit, I could too.

Anthropology

It was the first dance of ninth grade. I didn't know how to dance, so I figured I'd just stand there and watch; the girls and the band.

Minutes after kicking my boots off at the door, a girl asked me to dance. I wasn't sure I even knew who she was, then realized it was DeeDee Martin. She had changed over the summer.

She wore an oversize white T-shirt that fell below her hips, and obscured her shape. The song was slow so we couldn't just face each other and flail. I held her in my best wedding dance stance. I tottered out some stiff overthought steps, until she grew impatient and pulled me close.

We were belly to belly, and soon, pressed against her softness, biology raised its curious head. I pulled back like a cat over a washtub, but she just locked her hands behind my back and held me there.

I felt like a werewolf, a transformation was taking place and there was nothing I could do about it, but DeeDee didn't seem to mind.

My mother taught me to dance at weddings, counting out steps, leading me around, so I could gain confidence, get that rhythm down, suave and smooth like Dad wasn't.

Swaying against DeeDee to the beat of the music, I wondered, was this what she wanted? Was this what a slow dance was all about? That save the last dance for me thing? Maybe *it* was supposed to happen.

The world my mother prepared me for would never happen. The sixties burned it down. My generation danced alone, created our own shapes. It was about how the music made you feel, not a circle of steps, nothing to follow but the vibe, the music so loud we spoke with our bodies.

Seeing us dance, girls lined up to slow dance with me, the only boy on the floor. DeeDee let me in on a secret; music fast or slow, I could slow dance through it all, every song with every girl, 'til the lights came up and part way through the last song, find DeeDee and dance it to the end with her.

160 Carp

In early April carp were running up the creek to spawn. We were in eighth grade and spring filled us with the desire to fish. So, Friday afternoon, riding home on the bus, we dumped our books, grabbed our poles, and headed to The Point.

The Point was a long gravel spit where the creek entered the river, a flood-plain bounded by highlands on one side. About an eighth of a mile upstream, carp were stacked up below the falls, milling around in the stench of the swirling plunge pool.

Perry and Sweazy, Poinzy, Beej, and I, baited up with canned corn and doughballs. Within minutes everyone had a fish on, and it didn't let up all weekend. We ran home for lunch or supper, but otherwise we fished. It was a poor man's salmon run, all the excitement without the glamor of fly rods and wicker creels.

We were students of the carp; they were a step up from bullheads. As children, we concocted elaborate stink-baits in pickle jars to entice them. A twenty pounder could run downstream, empty your reel in a minute, and leave your twelve-pound test blowing in the breeze.

But it was a love-hate relationship. Carp were despised invaders, regardless of their esteem in Europe as a centerpiece of Christmas dinner. Here they muddied the water and destroyed the habitat of the natives, and we hated any invader like we hated ourselves for not being Indian, we the descendants of syphilitic, smallpox ridden assholes.

The DNR put a law on the books in the early '70s that powered our crusade. It became unlawful to return any rough fish, caught by angling, back into Minnesota waters. No longer was it a choice, it became illegal to show mercy.

As we fished, we kept Mom updated with our latest tally, 40, 80, 110. "What are you doing with all those fish?" she wanted to know. "We're throwing them in a pile in the woods, a big pile," like those turn of the century photographs: horizons of skinned bison carcasses, ducks, geese, pigeons, pike, deer, and elk hanging from railcars and tree-limbs, that intoxication of limitlessness and eradication so dear to the American heart.

"Merciful Heavens," Mom exclaimed.

By dusk on Sunday, we caught 160 carp and by midweek it was all a distant memory. But in nature nothing is forgotten. The sun grew stronger daily, and by Wednesday afternoon, the reek reached our house.

"What is that nasty smell?" Mom asked when I got home from school. She had a pretty good idea what it was, and I was in awe that our trophy was big enough to find us. Mom said it was an affront to the neighborhood. "But Mom," I argued, "What could we do? It's against the law to release them!"

"No law said you had to fish for them," Mom replied, "Nobody put a gun to your head. If you're not going to eat them what's the point of catching them?"

"But Mom they're destroying the habitat for smallmouth and walleye. The DNR wants us to, that's why it's a law!"

Mom said they were still living things and should be respected and not treated that way. She made me call my friends and pick out some shovels from the shed. Then she marched us down to the creek, like all the "good Germans" that Patton's 3rd army marched through Buchenwald, to see what had been done in their name.

Gagging, we dug a mass grave, deep enough to hold that maggoty, rotting, hip-high pile of fish and Mom stood there, arms crossed, smoking a cigarette, until all that remained was a fresh mound of dug dirt.

Hickeys Were Part of the Problem

Jackson Junior High. A single-story rectangle of red brick, sited on a forlorn tract of glacial outwash, surrounded by potato fields and alder swamp.

Miss Larson's English class. Three girls shipwrecked in a sea of twenty-six boys submerged in the most irresponsible throes of adolescent development, boys who'd known each other since kindergarten and had never been allowed in the same classroom since.

The sweet smell of dried illegal leaves purchased in the hallways and smoked around windswept corners of the building, mixed with a spirited cocktail of pituitary chemicals, plus Miss Larson, a sexy, unmarried, twenty-four-year-old first year instructor; heart brimming with ideals, neck bruised with hickeys.

Miss Larson could not control the class, and those hickeys were part of the problem.

The class snickered and whispered, gaining a deep hickey consciousness.

Bobby Buggs, seated in front, would raise his hand, and with a sugary voice ask,

"Miss Larson, what's that on your neck?" and the rumble of inattention held just below the surface would flood the room with an unshushable roar.

Miss Larson responded by wearing scarves and turtlenecks, but all Gary Glazner had to do was ask what was underneath, and the dam broke loose again. She yelled, she cried, but it usually required a visit from the principle to knock it back down.

Between classes or in study hall I would draw caricatures while other kids leaned on desks and watched. I'd been drawing since I could hold a pencil. It developed into a kind of performance art audience participation thing. They would make suggestions, and I would draw them. By sixth grade I had developed a set of stock characters. By eighth grade it was all about pushing boundaries.

It was before the bell and Miss Larson wasn't in the room yet. I was drawing and boys were shouting out suggestions. Having grown up in the aftermath of WWII, we were steeped in the lore of the Nazis, that ultimate evil. Thanks to *Hogan's Heroes*, running on a daily syndication at 5PM, Nazis were now funny too.

I'd drawn Nazis for years, doing what I thought Nazis did, holding submachine guns and saluting Hitler. The only other thing boys were obsessed with was sex. I could draw naked bodies and a withering array of veiny engorged male members in the most disgusting detail.

I like to believe there was nothing deeper in our choice of images that morning, nothing more than a random collection of suggestions and their painstaking transcription. Perhaps it began with that helmeted figure on hands and knees wearing a Gestapo tunic, but because he wore no trousers it is likely the tableau began with the uniformed and equally trouserless and swastikaed Nazi standing before him and coupled with him orally and in no time, we had a Teutonic threesome with the Nazi on his hands and knees in the middle taking it anatomically correctly from both ends.

Gary had just finished narrating for me, his vision of a woman drying her genitalia with a blow dryer. Holding it in his hands, he admired my faithful transcription on the flip-side of the Nazi triptych. That's when I noticed Miss Larson's face among the circle of onlookers surrounding my desk.

"Let me see that paper!" she said.

The class scattered like roaches in a flashlight beam, but Gary was pinned. She closed the emptied space between them, "Garret!" she demanded, "Give me that paper!"

In that instant we looked at each other and realized how unexplainable this drawing was and how unthinkable it would be if she got her hands on it. She grew in height as her shadow fell over him, and Gary backed away, shrinking beneath her, "No, Miss Larson...No... You can't..." as he balled it up between his fists.

She held out her open palm and repeated, "Garret, give me that paper!" and he pleaded, "No... Miss Larson, believe me...You can't!" she reached for his arm and in desperation, he hurled it over her head. I caught it, but, quick as a cat, she was on me: "Give me that paper!"

I threw it back to Gary. This wasn't like me, playing keep-away from a teacher. Miss Larson was furious and grabbed him.

"Eat it Gary..." I yelled.

Gary stuffed it into his mouth and started chewing, Miss Larson grabbed his cheeks between thumb and fingers, forced his jaws apart like a dog, and pulled the soggy ball from between his teeth.

The room fell silent as she walked back to her desk. She sat down, smoothed the crumpled thing flat with her palms, studied it for a moment, then folded it and placed it in an envelope. She licked it, sealed it, wrote something on it and asked one of the three girls to carry it down to the office.

The room was silent. The lesson began, and I was not surprised when a student office volunteer showed up with a pass ordering Gary and I down to the office. There was nothing to do but go, no explanations, no brainstorm, no angle.

We stood before the principal's desk. It was Friday afternoon. He handed us each a sealed envelope with photocopies of our drawings and instructed us to give them to our parents, who would be required to come with us on Monday morning for a meeting.

Tilt-A-Whirl

I was going on a scout camp that weekend, leaving in the evening, so I couldn't drag it out over the weekend. I had to tell Mom before I left, before Dad got home from work. Mom usually got her hair done on Friday afternoons, so I sat waiting with the dreaded envelope until she returned from the beauty shop.

I told Mom I got in trouble in school. That I'd drawn a picture that was pretty bad and was supposed to show her. She asked what it was, and I told her about the three Nazis and their sexual encounter. She said she didn't need to see it; said she'd talk to Dad about it over the weekend. I stuck that envelope in my underwear drawer and went to camp.

On Monday morning, Gary was in the office. His mom had to work and couldn't come. She signed his copy, and on the phone said she didn't see what the big deal was anyway, Gary hadn't even drawn it. The principle asked Mom if she'd seen my drawing and to my surprise she lied and said she had.

Then there was no reason to look at it, he said, as long as we were all aware of the content. The principal said he wasn't saying there was anything wrong with it. There was a time and a place for everything, but he didn't think school was the place for this.

I was shocked. A place for this?

That night I was sitting in the kitchen, doing some homework, when Dad walked in and said, "I just need to know one thing...You like girls, right?"

The Grizzly Adams of Advertising

In an era before logos were art,

plastered across every shirt, jacket, and cap,

Back when all that unclaimed ad space was wilderness,

vast and unexploited,

Dad noticed me wearing a T-shirt

from a car dealership.

Across my chest the logo read,

"Baseball, Hotdogs, Apple Pie, and Chevrolet."

"How much are they paying you to wear that shirt?"
he asked.

Whenever Dad asked a question like that I got pissed off,

What I wanted to say was "Fuck You."

Instead, I said,

"Nothing. Why would they pay me. It's a shirt, I got it for free."

"That's prime advertising space," Dad said

"It covers your heart.

They should pay you

to wear it."

"They gave me a shirt." I replied. "I didn't have to buy it."

"That isn't enough."

Dad said.

Hiking Merit Badge

The summer between ninth and tenth grades, Sweazy and I devised a plan that served a dual purpose. Earlier that year, we were busted at a weekend church camp breaking several commandments, and a few federal laws, most serious being in possession of cannabis and alcohol. We now existed under increased parental scrutiny, facing privations of freedom and trust.

I had a girlfriend I met that winter at a party. She went to a different school and lived in a trailer park in Coon Rapids. The occasions I saw her were few and our relationship consisted of long nightly phone calls that Mom hated because the line was always busy and no one could get through.

We were still in Boy Scouts, a condition we kept on the down-low: green uniforms with little badges sewn on them, definitely not cool.

Perhaps showing a renewed interest in the path to Eagle Scout would lower our parents' suspicions.

Hannah's trailer park home was ten miles away, and the return trip made it a neat twenty; coincidentally, a requirement for Hiking Merit Badge. There were shorter hikes required, fives and tens, to warm you up for the big twenty. But I didn't need a warmup, a girl was waiting at the end of the trail.

Mr. Haugen was the counselor for hiking merit badge. Instead of calling to officially register, we decided to tell him later. Perhaps we doubted the legitimacy of the destination, and the unlikely terrain we'd traverse to reach it.

It was unorthodox; hiking, at its core, was an inspiring journey through nature, exploring its roadless reaches, unspoiled vistas, possible only on foot.

Our route eked through some of the most soul crushing strip-mall sprawl in Anoka County, flat, featureless, and heavily trafficked. I was convinced the letter of the law would prevail. I'd been to the Boundary Waters, had seen plenty of pristine forests. Perhaps it was time to appreciate a humbler landscape, closer to home, eliminate the use of fossil fuels, a truer Daniel Boone.

It being a weekday, Hannah's mother was at work. Without packs or walking sticks, Sweazy and I set off, not even hats to shade our feathered hair. We stopped at the store to buy a pack of Marlboros, lit up and started walking. Nothing in our appearance betrayed us as scouts.

We crossed the Mighty Mississippi, crossed the Rum, cut through downtown Anoka, and picked up Coon Rapids Boulevard. We left the sidewalks behind and entered that no-man's land of ditches; an eco-system of pigweed, turkey-foot, and road-salt. It felt stupid to walk and not hitch-hike, but By-Golly, we were scouts.

Hannah told us to watch for landmarks: a Kinney Shoe store, a derelict motel sign. She said when we saw the gravel-pit we were almost there. We found the trailer-court and located her trailer. Once inside, I abandoned Sweazy to the TV and joined Hannah in her bedroom. I was finally there. She removed her bra and we dry-humped 'til we were sore, our lips chapped, then re-emerged to the light of the TV, faces blotched, eyes bleared.

After a can of coke and a goodbye kiss, we got back on the trail before her mother could return from work and catch us.

The way home required no compass, no checking for moss on the north side of a tree, but it wasn't a trudge either; the fast-food lights and come-ons of commerce; this brash new wilderness of possibility held more allure than the sanctity of the forest. Crossing the weed-cracked asphalt, this trash strewn frontier of ditch and median, I felt autonomy: If I did the time and walked the walk, nobody was gonna tell me what kind of scenery to enjoy.

After a few weeks of procrastination, I walked over to Sweazy's, and he called Mr. Haugen. I don't remember how it was that he made the call, or why I sat in the living room while he spoke on the phone in the hallway. I tried to mask my doubts with a casual air, hoping the call was a formality. I heard Sweazy's muffled voice around the corner, then he walked back into the room. The conversation had been too short.

"Well?"

Sweazy described the response, not skepticism but anger: What kind of crap were we trying to pull? Our ploy was transparent; that was embarrassing, but to receive no credit? Well that sucked. In the end, we both became Eagle Scouts, but we never earned a badge for hiking.

Mill Pond 1975

Stoned teens flipping off

the rope-swing's farthest arc,

somersaulting through the sky,

limbs cocked and crazy,

splashing in,

like thrown stones,

sinking into the dark, muffled silence,

suspended near bottom,

like a fish;

motionless,

deep water cold,

silt squishing between toes.

That moment is forever,

bubbles rising,

air in your lungs the compass,

and you rise too,

kick for the surface,

then burst through,

into the the light,

into the the screaming and laughter.

You're a stoned teen,

your tired world

is new

again.

Men's Room Reflections

Where I grew up,
mirrors in the men's room were scratched out,
smashed into spiderwebs of shattered glass;
a feelings' fractured expression.

It was tough for a boy to see.

A man's image inspired violence,
damage, mutilation, disfigurement;
destruction was an act of self-preservation.
Nothing worth looking at.

Junebug

It was after we'd drained the bottle of Southern Comfort, long after Poinzy somehow knocked over a Pepsi canister at the pool hall. We fled, out of town, driving aimlessly in Dad's newly painted Chevy Impala, looking for a party, anywhere we could land. Poinzy was stuffed in the backseat, head hanging out the rear window like a yellow lab, a trail of puke jet-streamed down Dad's indigo quarter-panel.

We pulled into a parking space outside Super America. I was scrubbing off all evidence of vomit with a gas-station squeegee. High-school folk-wisdom wove a cautionary tale of puke eating through any enamel less than 6 months old.

Poinzy sat on the running-board, the passenger door swung open wide, head hung between his knees, thick strings of saliva connecting him to the compact puddle of bile he'd heaved onto the oil-stained concrete.

An elderly couple parked beside the spot where Poinzy, wracked with hiccups and dry-heaves, contemplated the depths of his plumbing. As they passed between the cars, she turned to her husband and shook her head with compassion,

"Isn't that sad?" she said.

It was Friday night, 11:00 PM, moths and June bugs threw themselves against the fluorescent lights in a mistaken quest for the moon.

Parental Advice

It was the Homecoming dance and cold; we hadn't even watched the game. I was passed out with the spins in the backseat of Sweazy's Dodge Polara.

I was drawing too much attention; forehead-down on one of the tables surrounding the gymnasium dance floor, so Julayne and Sweazy were forced to haul me outside. Sweazy came out periodically to warm up the car and have a smoke. Julayne, my girlfriend, was worried I might freeze to death, all scrunched up in my jean jacket.

When the dance was over and I hadn't recovered, Sweazy drove me to Julayne's house. Her mother was at the VFW on a date with an off-duty Anoka cop. I collapsed on the sofa in front of the TV, too sick to raise my head.

The VFW was down the street and around midnight her mother came home and rousted me off the couch. Her boyfriend was standing by the kitchen door, avoiding the whole thing. I guess that's how off-duty cops handled domestic situations. She towered over me and scoffed,

"What were you drinking!?"

"Brandy." I replied.

"What kind of Brandy!?"

"Five-Star."

"That's why you're sick," she said, "you bought my daughter cheap liquor! Never buy my daughter cheap liquor!"

Tripping by the Bridge

I stood on the gravel, at the party spot by the bridge. Cars pulled into a circle like covered wagons. We leaned against fenders smoking, shaggy teen-aged boys in leather coats, older ones too; dropped out or graduated.

A joint laced with something and passed on, a bitter taste in the back of my throat. MDA or a pig tranquilizer.

I took another hit and passed the joint back to Mitch Riedel, who passed it to his girlfriend. I was getting pretty high and felt like going, and there was Rory's station wagon, the backdoor open, so I climbed in.

Creaking over the potholes and onto the road, music so loud I could hardly sit up. Feeling a fast corner, I slid onto the floor like a square of Jello off a cafeteria tray.

Wedged between seats, ass on the differential hump, I stared up through the window; watching the clouds, telephone poles, tree-tops, all flashing past.

In time Rory must have slowed down, pulled over, and turned off the engine. It was quiet now. Just treetops and crickets chirping.

Craig Cahill opened my door, peered inside and the whole car vanished into his hand, and there I was lying on the gravel by the bridge, shocked and surprised, looking up at a ring of perplexed faces, bent down, looking at me.

A Scout is Reverent

To be awarded the Eagle Scout rank, merit badges must be earned, tasks accomplished, officers and arbiters of the community signing off on one's compliance and moral character.

I had collected most of the signatures I needed, all but an officer of the church who would vouch for my reverence, one of the twelve scout laws.

I never found drug use, heavy metal, or premarital sex in conflict with reverence. Our family attended church less often, since that incident at church camp in 9th grade where we were caught breaking the commandments pertaining to sex, drugs, and alcohol. My mother felt sufficiently shunned by the congregation, allowing us to sleep in on Sundays.

I assumed it would be a formality, stopping off at the church office for a polite flourish of the pen, but the pastor wanted to come by the house to discuss it.

Mom didn't like the sound of it. Was my reverence in question? Would more misdeeds come to light? Ministers only visit troubled homes and the last time our house was visited had been a shaming, soul-wrenching prayer fest, seeking guidance and forgiveness from the Holy Spirit.

On the day of his visit, Mom baked cookies and set the table for a luncheon. We paced the kitchen as the appointed hour approached. Mom asked if there was something the pastor knew that she didn't? A reason for the house-call? I knew there were many things she didn't know about, suspicions the community at large held about my appearance and behavior.

When the pastor came to the door, Mom asked him to sit down at the table, but he abruptly announced he wanted to speak with me privately, perhaps we could go to my bedroom. Mom's face paled.

I led him down the hallway to my bedroom and shut the door. I sat on the bed, and he sat on the chair. It was weird, probably the first time any adult beside a parent or babysitter had sat in my room. He looked around, ashtrays full of cigarette butts, beer can collection on the shelf. Did he wish to observe me in my natural habitat? The posters covering my walls indeed told the story.

There were fluorescent mind-tripping psychedelic optical illusions, blood-shot eyeballs, color photos of Jimmy Page and Mick Jagger, a cartoon image of a Yaqui medicine man about to ingest a mind-altering mushroom.

Elbows on his knees, he got straight to the point, told me there were rumors and stories circulating about parties, drinking, and drug use. He wanted to give me a chance to defend myself, to confess.

I took a moment to collect my thoughts. This was more direct than I'd expected. It seemed ludicrous to ask. The truth was hanging tacked and taped to the walls around us. Was this rhetorical? Was he going to let me answer and then produce documents to refute me?

As a child I had witnessed firsthand the Saturday night/Sunday morning dichotomies of the Lutheran congregation, watched President Nixon lie to the nation about his involvement with Watergate, and so I looked him straight in the eyes, and said,

"I don't do that anymore."

Postcard from the Bicentennial Summer

We were almost seventeen,

walking across a park,

throwing firecrackers

in the grass.

A cop appeared

over the hill,

took our Black-Cats and

ordered us to

empty our pockets

onto a picnic table.

Alongside my pocketknife,

some change, and a book of matches,

I laid down my favorite pipe,

and a nickel bag of weed.

He said "Leave those two

and take the rest."

We walked off,

spared, yet cheated.

Convinced the crime was

in the bag, I turned,

asked if he'd give my pipe back,

said I had a sentimental

attachment.

He nearly tossed it my way,

then scowled,

swatted at me and said,

"Get outta here!"

I Never Wanted to Be That Guy

Rory, Sweazy and I had been in school together since kindergarten, been in cub scouts, slept over at each other's houses on Friday nights, built models and watched war movies on TV. As we got older it became smoking cigarettes, watching *The Midnight Special* and sneaking booze from somebody's dad.

Rory was the first to get into drugs. Puberty hit him hard and fast, by the end of seventh grade he was doing acid, in eighth grade his dark hair was greasy and long and he was sleeping through class, in ninth grade his parents pulled him out of school and put him in treatment.

I didn't see him again until tenth grade. We were in the new high school and our lockers were nearby. He asked if I still played guitar. He'd played drums since sixth grade, but said he was taking guitar lessons, studying theory. We started playing together and became friends again.

We started a band, took it pretty seriously, practiced at least three nights a week, sometimes more. First it was Rory and me, then it got to the point where we wanted a bass player. Sweazy played guitar, he'd taken piano lessons in grade school, and he worked construction with his old man so he had the money to invest in a bass guitar and amp.

We practiced in Rory's basement for a couple years then moved into my basement to give his parents a break from the floor rattling din. Rory still had the drum-kit, but preferred the guitar, so we had to find a drummer.

Denny Van Kampen lived up on Indian Mound Road. He was a hyper-active little guy a couple years younger than us with a dent sunk in the middle of his chest right where you'd think his heart should be. One night he came over to bum cigarettes while we were playing, sat down behind that empty drum-set, and By God he could keep a beat. I'd never seen him do a thing in his life except light fires in dry grass, and here he was, without a lesson, moving two legs and two arms independently of each other.

Denny was known for his dorky pranks but was always there for practice and became our default drummer. Mr. Van Kampen was happy that Denny had found a place in our off-beat underground world and showed his gratitude by giving us beers, letting us smoke, and talking to us like adults.

Most nights Mr. Van Kampen was down at the Legion club across the field from their house. If we went down there for a hamburger there was a good chance he'd buy us a beer.

It was a Friday night and we stopped by the legion on our way to a party. There was a cowboy band playing. Denny's dad was excited and said we were lucky to be there. This guy was famous, and he would introduce us, musician to musician. We were long haired rock'n'rollers, only here because they wouldn't card our underage asses, and these guys were old, wearing white cowboy hats and didn't look like they'd wanna talk to anybody like us.

It's not like I didn't appreciate country music. It's what our dads listened to in the garage. It was the soundtrack to every beer-joint in town. We had guitars in common, but it hardly seemed like the same instrument, they played theirs with the volume so low and so un-distorted you could hear what they actually sang.

The band was on break and Mr. Van Kampen introduced us to the singer from his stool at the end of the bar. I can't remember the guy's name, just that he had white hair and smoked Marlboro Lights. He'd been playing since the early '50s, said he was a regular on the Saturday Night Barn Dance, and played various local radio shows with musicians I'd never heard of. His successes were as old as the black and white promotional photo he autographed for me: a younger man dressed in a fringed western suit and white Stetson. He'd signed, "As seen on KSTP Channel 5" above his signature, about as vital to me as the Gene Autry show dad watched on Sunday mornings.

I left that night with his photo in my hand and taped it up on my bedroom wall next to Jimmy Page, though I don't remember why. In 1976, 1958 felt like another era, and it was, but I see now as a matter of years it wasn't many. He was still living it. We chuckled about him grasping at his local fame. We were different and always would be. He was the past. We were the future.

Coming of Age

Mom sat up most nights with her romance novels, drinking coffee. No matter what time I came in, she was waiting. I was expected to make conversation, tell her how my night had been. Usually, I prepared an anecdote or two, careful to stay beyond range of her sensitive nose, and hope I wasn't betrayed by my psychoactive state. I attempted a coherent nonchalance, stretched my arms and yawned, suggesting it was time for bed.

There were the nights, that unsteadily, I made it down the hallway to my room, to lie in bed with the spins. Then the realization that the merry-go-round wasn't over, that I would need to spend some time on the cool tile of the bathroom floor. Praying my gastrointestinal distress would not disturb the silence of the night, I continued to believe my adventures were concealed.

Our high school rock band relocated from Rory's basement to mine. I can't remember the impetus of the move. I know Rory's younger sister was tired of the noise, and unimpressed with the quality of the boys involved.

Perhaps Rory's parents looked forward to watching television without the volume blaring. In those days before remotes, volume control required a walk across the room. My parents, on the other hand, were probably happy to know my whereabouts three or four nights a week, and nothing could distract them from another night with *Columbo*.

I'd already been suspended for smoking cigarettes in school, so a basement full of chain-smoking teens wasn't a problem, but the first night someone came down the stairs carrying a case of Old Milwaukee, I was stunned. We'd been doing this at Rory's for over a year, but that was Rory's. He'd given his parents a wild ride since seventh grade, to them beer was a relief.

Our TV was in the living room, you had to pass through to reach the basement stairs.

Jake Douglas set the jingling carton of bottles on the table and dropped his leather jacket on the floor. "Did you carry that by my parents?" I asked.

"Yeah."

"You talked to 'em?"

"Yeah."

"They didn't say anything?"

"Nope."

"Wow." Upstairs, the TV droned on, another plot unraveled. I reached for a bottle.

Joining the Tribe

Since spring, Charlene and I had been pursuing a process hobbled by obstacles, logistical misunderstandings, a failure of mechanics. But here we were, at the drive-in movie-triple feature, finally, losing our virginity.

Behind the wheel of my Chevy Bel Air, windows fogged with condensation, I pulled up my Levi's. Charlene was on the passenger side, fumbling with a more complicated arrangement of undergarments. I left her to it, got out and lit a smoke.

Rory sat on the hood of his car, parked beside mine, his back against the windshield, drinking an Old Milwaukee.

I jumped up next to him without a word, and he handed me a bottle. I leaned back and watched the movie.

Rory's door opened. Donna climbed out and lit a cigarette. This was routine for them. She buttoned her jacket and pulled the collar against her throat. I could see her breath. She crossed her arms and said, "You guys do it?"

"Yup," I replied.

"Where's Charlene?"

I nodded toward my car and Charlene's shape, huddled inside.

"What's wrong with you!?" she scolded. "You get back in that car and you sit with her."

I shrugged, hopped down, and did as I was told.

Coat Pile

It was a party at Butch and Benny's. They lived in a duplex past the Elk Lake Pavilion. There were mostly bikers at their parties, and a few of their old ladies. There weren't many single girls, but optimism is a beer's best buddy.

It was winter, nothing doing outside, just the straight line from the front door through the living room, into the kitchen, down the stairs to the basement, where a cover band played, then back up the stairs, repeated like an infinity of mirrors until the consumption of alcohol and drugs finally brought you down like a tranquilized hyena on *Mutual of Omaha's Wild Kingdom*.

I was standing beside the pile of coats heaped in the corner to the left of the door when the futility hit me along with the cumulative effect of all that keg-beer. The coat-pile called me down and I passed out.

I awoke and realized I wasn't alone. Someone lay next to me in that pile of coats, our backs touching. The thrum of bass and drum vibrated the floor beneath us. Fresh from unconsciousness, I could feel her slow breathing, and with eyes closed, I turned to face her. She found me and we embraced. I couldn't believe my luck. Her lips searched for mine and it was then, as our tongues probed, I noticed what felt like whiskers around her mouth.

Our eyes opened together and I realized she was a bearded drunk in a flannel shirt, and without another thought, like something choreographed, we rolled apart and lying back-to-back once more, resumed our separate dreams.

Finding the Faithful Pony Within

It usually worked, getting behind the wheel of a car, turning the key in the ignition, checking the mirrors and putting it in gear. But tonight, Sweazy and I were tripping.

Hands on the wheel, I could see the interior of my '63 Chevy perfectly, every detail of the red steel dashboard and green glowing radium dials. But looking through the windows all I could see was black, like someone had covered the entire car with a tarp.

We were parked on the side of the road in front of Butch and Benny's, pointed south, that much I knew. Sweazy said all he could see were giant pink spider-webs, so he was no help. I eased the car into first and made a decision: start driving and see what happens.

My destination was home, and like a psychedelic version of stories grandma told about drunks passed out on horseback, homeward bound from the saloon, l begged the horse-power under the hood to please get me there.

I felt gravel turn to blacktop, sensed miles moving beneath us, saw myself making turns and changing gears, it was all working, and I wasn't sure why. I knew the sound of hitting something could signal a fault in my strategy and tuned all remaining senses cat whisker sharp, braced for the slightest impact.

Sweazy sat shotgun, gaze forward, pursued an all-consuming interior monologue with radioscopic awareness. His lack of concern boosted my confidence. I convinced myself he could see through the spiderwebs and like a seeing-eye dog, would sing out if I went astray.

After one significant righthand turn, I found myself idling, transmission in neutral. I looked over at Sweazy and feeling it was the right thing to do, turned off the ignition. In that instant the windows cleared and through them I saw the peeling white paint of my parents' garage door .

A Civics Lesson

This was the first time I'd ever seen it. I was told it happened in remote, impoverished countries behind the Iron Curtain, but not in our town.

We were down at The Point, where Elm Creek joins the Mississippi, a carload of boys parked by a frozen river, tripping their brains out on LSD. Bottles of Cold Duck were being passed around, lit joints too. The windows were frosted over and I was just losing the power of language, when I heard a knock on the window.

Poinzy rolled it down and a belch of smoke sucked into the sub-zero night, obliterating the features of the cop who shined his flashlight into each of our cow-eyed faces. I was strangely comforted by the realization that I could never talk my way out of this; our crimes so obvious, I could just relax.

Another squad car pulled up when Luke opened the passenger door, got out, and offered the nearest cop his I.D. With a clear voice he announced his name and stated, "I believe you know my father, Wendell Calloway, on the city council..." and before I could fully marvel at his ability to open a door, those cops had briskly climbed back into their cars and driven off, leaving us in stunned silence.

In that icy hour of the new year, I realized my father's name would never get me out of anything.

Between the Lines in '79

I was driving west on Highway 10.

Minutes earlier I'd been lounging in Tony's green Monte Carlo, smoking hashish in the parking lot of Thumpers nightclub, after seeing Commander Cody- and His Lost Planet Airmen.

It was a warm summer night, mid-week, long after last call, alone on an empty road. I'd only drunk one beer during the show, but now trying to hold it between the white lines and keep my speed above 40, I realized how stoned I was.

Soon I noticed the steady presence of headlights in my rearview mirror. I told myself it wasn't a cop, but the lights just stayed there and that was a worry.

Speeding up made it harder to stay between the lines. It was taking all the concentration I had. Then I'd realize I was below 40 again, speed up, and those headlights still wouldn't pass. I felt like I was steering a pinball.

When the Ferry Street exit came up, I blinkered right, hoping to escape, but beneath the streetlights, I saw a sheriff followed me up. A few blocks later the cherries snapped on.

After pulling over, I felt I should show some respect, let him witness my deep sense of responsibility. So instead of waiting for him to approach me like a petulant child, I opened my door and strode back to greet him in his squad car. I wanted him to know I shared his interest. I truly wanted to get to the bottom of whatever prompted him to pull me over.

He told me I'd crossed a white line at the exit and asked me to take a seat next to him on the passenger side.

He studied my license and asked how much I'd had to drink. For once I didn't need to lie, his question had nothing to do with smoke. He pulled out his flashlight, shined the beam in my eyes, then turned it off. We sat together quietly, chatter from the police radio rippling the dome-lit darkness.

Holding my license between thumb and forefinger, he absently tapped its edge on his knee and gazed into the night. My focus remained on him. He shined the flashlight in my eyes again and continued to tap my license against his leg. Then he asked how far I had to drive.

"A mile and a half." I replied with conviction. He pondered a few moments longer, tapped my license on his knee one last time, and handed it back.

"Go home." he said.

Wrecked

I got a job pumping gas at the Fina station in Osseo. Not exactly what I was looking for, but besides being a rockstar, I had no ideas. I wanted my mother off my back, needed money for gas and beer, car insurance, and more records.

Pumping gas was way more glamorous than my last job; bagging hundred-pound gunny-sacks on a potato farm and eating baloney sandwiches for lunch.

I started out on the day shift, the era of full service; I pumped gas, checked fluids, and washed windows.

The building was a cinderblock, two-stall garage, that stepped up into an office with a raw plank floor, one bathroom and a back room for overstock. In place of a cash register, we used a cigarette-burned wooden cashbox and a spiral notebook to register each sale. We counted out the change. A new-fangled microwave sat above the chest freezer to zap those pukey smelling chuck-wagon sandwiches.

There was no Clean Air Act; smoking inside the station was encouraged as an alternative to smoking near the pumps. Fina's cash-cow was cheap cigarettes; they cost fifty-five cents a pack and nurtured a devoted clientele.

Pumping gas didn't pay, but there were perks. One was guaranteed gasoline during the Oil Embargo, another was a chance to flirt with girls. We were the dregs of the baby boom, just entering the world as the great post-war miracle collapsed around us: the fall of Vietnam, inflation, recession, rising unemployment.

Each morning as the nightshift ended down the road at Spancrete, a bunch of guys I knew from high school came in for smokes on their way to the liquor store. Kids I'd known since grade school, their faces grubby, radiating anger and despair. The music that moved a generation, rang like a bell without a clapper.

Jan, our manager, was a perky, bespectacled tomboy who dressed in oversized coveralls that only made her cuter. Her mother-hen approach inspired a fierce loyalty. The assistant-manager was a bodybuilder with a muscle-car, who subsisted on the lean hamburger he weighed out by the pound on a Weight Watchers scale.

When he quit, I was the only possible replacement. I'd been an Eagle Scout and was going to community college, not the worst bet. I took the job, and for an extra buck an hour, worked weeknights three to close with an odious six-thirty opener on Saturday and Sunday mornings.

I became Fina's off-hours face. When applications for employment were filed, my recommendations carried weight. Our ranks were soon filled with friends and family; a shaggy army of stoners and underachievers; and one of these was Sweazy, my childhood pal.

In the frigid winter of '79, Fina's regional office directed us to push Heet; that little plastic bottle of isopropyl alcohol you dumped in your tank to battle gas-line freeze. We grew up in Minnesota, our parents never used Heet. and their cars sat outside all night.

Instructed to peddle a lie and make a buck for a corporation chafed at Sweazy's conscience. He despised ignorance, and if customers were stupid enough to buy placebos, he felt compelled to profit on the side.

At the beginning of each shift, Sweazy would sell one bottle of Heet, dump it in their tank, and toss the empty bottle in the trash. When the customer drove away, he fished out the bottle, filled it with gasoline, brought it inside and set it back on the shelf with the other fifteen bottles.

When the next customer appeared, he reached up for that same bottle, and emptied it in their tank.

Throughout the shift he repeated his subterfuge, keeping careful track of how many times he sold that bottle, and at the end, removed his proceeds from the till. The scheme appeared foolproof; there wasn't a record of any sale, but that was the problem. It was cold and every other shift was selling Heet in record quantities.

On New Year's Eve, Sweazy and I split a hit of mescaline around ten o'clock. We sought consolation in the hours before those mythical New Year's kisses would be unleashed upon us, mistletoe tacked above every doorway. We went out searching for that raucous archetypal party, an island of light in our adolescent darkness.

We were standing in the aisle of a White Castle, chatting with a table of people we recognized from high school when the drug's terrible consciousness reared up within us, the din fell suddenly silent.

I looked up, the whole restaurant had stopped eating and was focused on us. I glanced at our classmates; they were staring too. I wondered; did I really know them?

Without goodbyes, we fled to the parking lot, escaped in Sweazy's turquoise Nova. Between the windchill and our startling loss of social skills, the night became less welcoming.

There wasn't much snow that winter, just cold. I don't remember choosing to drive on Lake George, but where else do you go when you're tripping your balls off and still live at home.

We spent the next six hours ensconced in darkness, driving in large loose circles, car spinning across the ice like an empty bottle. At one point we came upon the wreckage of a fish house, splintered into kindling, scattered beneath our headlights.

Had we done it? I got out, inspected the bumper for damage, ran my palms across the cold chrome, meticulously, but found no evidence.

This left two possibilities: first, that the wreck of the fish house was a shared hallucination, not lying there at our feet. The second, was more chilling; others were out there like us in that immense eternity, driving aimlessly, with great conviction, faces illuminated greenly by the dashboard dials.

But beyond our awareness, moments were gathering into minutes, gradually forming hours. The darkness withdrew into shapes; shadows and grays, finally retreating into dawn. Riddles were scattered, mysteries vanished, it was a new year and time to return for the morning shift at Fina.

On the way off the lake, Sweazy spied a pair of fishermen crouched on buckets in the distance. Getting closer, we realized it was a father and son, doing something wholesome on that first day of the year.

Periodically the fishermen glanced in our direction. Sweazy maintained a steady speed, closing on their position, eyes intent.

"You really gonna do this?" I asked. He didn't answer.

As we neared them, the fishermen rose to their feet, standing nervously beside their buckets. When we were close enough to read their expressions, they bolted.

The father, in a paternal feint, ran in a direction opposite the boy, like a rabbit or bird drawing a predator's attention from its' offspring. Bearing down on the father with a final burst of speed, Sweazy swung right, veered off the lake, and bounced onto the road.

Jan had shrewdly volunteered to do the inventory that morning, allowing us a late start. 1980 emerged battleship gray.

We tried to be casual as she slipped into her coat and gathered her belongings. We seemed to be talking okay, but Sweazy wasn't saying much. I monitored Jan's expressions closely but noticed no cues of alarm. I did notice how large and luminescent everyone's teeth had become, aglow like foggy moons eclipsing their purple lips.

The first car pulled up to the pumps. "Sweazy," Jan suggested, "Could you get that one?"

Sweazy approached the driver, bending slightly to receive his instructions. Then he walked back inside, and just stood there.

"What happened?" she asked, "What's wrong?"

"I can't do it." he replied from somewhere, maybe the depths of his soul, "I just can't do it."

I ran out, pumped the perplexed man's gas and returned for damage control. I wasn't sure what Sweazy offered in my absence, but found only silence.

"Are you guys gonna be all right?" Jan asked. "I gotta pick up my dad and get him over to my sister's, for brunch."

I assured her, we were fine. She left, reluctantly, face wrapped in doubt.

After a couple Chuck-wagons and a coke, the world stopped being new. As the heightened awareness deserted our bodies, we limped into the afternoon, emptied and numb, each moment endless. At about three, when the next shift appeared, we climbed into his car and drove away.

We hadn't been home yet, there was no reason to go there now, brains wrung out like sponges by the mescaline.

We left Osseo, seeking refuge on a day every bit as scary as a Sunday. We washed up in Coon Rapids, at McDonald's, with a panoramic view of Anoka-Ramsey Junior College. It was a nightmare. The irony that our trip began in a White Castle and ended at McDonald's, highlighted everything that was wrong with my life.

Slouched in that yellow Formica booth, nursing a coke, I knew Sweazy was right. I couldn't do it anymore either.

About the Author

Scott Vetsch lives and works as a carpenter in Minneapolis, Minnesota. He remodels historic homes. A University of Minnesota alum with a B.A. in English Literature, he is an avid reader, participant, and supporter of the literary community. He is a founding member of the Bosso Poetry Company, which has been performing spoken word, music, and poetry in and around the Twin Cities since back in the twentieth century. He is an avid outdoorsman and Eagle scout; ecology is his religion. He still lives by the same river he grew up on, fishes it when he can, and crosses it daily.

www.ingramcontent.com/pod-product-compliance
Lightning Source LLC
Chambersburg PA
CBHW032225080426
42735CB00008B/713